THE FIGHT GAME

THE
FIGHT GAME

BY

James & Frank Butler

WITH 12 PAGES
OF PLATES

LONDON 1956

THE SPORTSMANS BOOK CLUB

This Sportsmans Book Club edition was produced in 1956
for sale to its members only. Full details of SBC are
obtainable from the proprietors, Phœnix House Ltd., 38
William IV Street, London, W.C.2., and at Letchworth
Garden City, Hertfordshire. The book is set in 10 on
12 pt. Times New Roman, and has been reprinted by
Morrison & Gibb Ltd., at Edinburgh. It was first
published by The World's Work (1913) Ltd. in 1954.

To our old friend
NAT FLEISCHER
boxing's greatest ambassador

CONTENTS

ILLUSTRATIONS

FOREWORD

JACK DEMPSEY
Former Heavyweight Champion of the World

WHEN JIMMY AND FRANK BUTLER asked me to write a few words as a foreword to their new book which covers nearly sixty years of boxing in many parts of the world, I assured them it would be a great honour. You see, I have known the Butlers for nearly thirty years, and consider them to be among my best English friends.

I had heard of Jimmy long before I was to win the heavyweight championship from Jess Willard in 1919. I met him for the first time when as champion I paid a visit, accompanied by the late Damon Runyon, to England in the early twenties. I boxed a charity exhibition against Phil Scott, the British champion at the time, and against Eddie Eagan, for the Sussex County Hospital at the Dome in Brighton for my dear friend, that great sportsman, the late Sir Harry Preston. Frank was then a slip of a schoolboy, but he had a front seat at the ringside!

It was more than twenty years later that I met the Butlers again (although we had corresponded regularly), and it took a war to bring us together again. I was in London, a Lieutenant-Commander in the U.S. Coast Guard, when they both looked me up and added a warm glow to some dreary nights while London was blacked out.

I caught up with the Butlers again in 1946 when father and son flew to New York to cover the Joe Louis—Billy Conn heavyweight championship for their newspapers. On June 24 I was celebrating my fifty-first birthday quietly at the Great Northern Hotel in New York City. I heard the Butlers were in town and invited them round for a quiet breakfast, and to talk again of old times.

Jimmy knows the fight game from A to Z, and from Z to A. He is respected on both sides of the Atlantic, and Frank has done a swell job following in his dad's steps. I believe it is true to say Frank has almost as many friends in America as he has in his own country.

Between them they have a wealth of boxing stories, and it is with great pleasure that I hand you over with the highest recommendation to *The Fight Game*.

JACK DEMPSEY.

HOLLYWOOD, CALIFORNIA, 1935.

INTRODUCTION

MY SON FRANK was little more than a baby when I first took him round the training camps of all the great champions. Some folk said I was introducing him to a tough racket much too early in life, but isn't life itself a tough racket, and can anybody really be blooded too early?

In my heart I wanted him to become a sports writer from the day he was born. That's why I took him to meet Jack Dempsey when Dempsey first came to England. I took him to watch Ted Kid Lewis in action and to the training camps of Augie Ratner and Mickey Walker (in preparation for the Tommy Milligan world title fight in 1927). I used to slip him into the National Sporting Club and take him to the tougher arenas like Premierland and the Blackfriars Ring.

I never mentioned anything definitely about sports writing to him, but he knew what he wanted to be, and his destiny seemed to be carved when at the age of twelve, I had a whimsical complaint from one of the Marist Fathers teaching him languages at St. Mary's College.

"Your son is hopeless at Latin and French," said his language master, "and what is more, he isn't interested in these subjects, having the audacity to inform me that he is concentrating entirely on English as he is going to be a sports writer!"

My face reflected the concern that seemed necessary, but in my heart I was delighted. The last time I sat down to write a book on boxing was a long time ago. Frank had just joined the *Daily Express*, so I dedicated my effort to him, hoping that one day he would become a top sports writer. That wish was fulfilled many years ago, but now another ambition of mine has been realised. We have written this book on boxing which I think deals adequately with the greatest champions of more than five decades.

PART ONE

ONCE UPON A TIME

BY

JAMES BUTLER

CHAPTER I

WHEN BOXING WAS REALLY TOUGH

FOR FIFTY-FIVE YEARS I have occupied a ringside seat watching with some excitement new champions crowned, often shaking my head a little sadly as one of the old masters, unable to cheat the inevitable twilight, wilts before the energy and stamina of less artistic but younger foes. I began using my own fists with an amateur club in South-East London, St. James's A.C., then I became a time-keeper and later I refereed many bouts in which champions took part in London, Liverpool and Manchester. So perhaps I will be forgiven when I stroke my grey beard and chuckle just a little when I listen to tough stories about gangsters and gun-men of the modern ring.

Gun-men barely exist in boxing to-day . . . that is, not outside of Hollywood and the imagination of those "Appointment-with-Fear" authors who write to chill the spine or curdle the blood. There are plenty of racketeers in the fight game—particularly in America, but these spiv-characters must not be mistaken as sinister killers slouching round training camps, dressing rooms and at the ringside ready to press a trigger and transfer the fighter who dares to disobey into the next world.

The U.S. racketeers are gamblers and shady characters who would not hesitate to bribe or fix a fight. They are the undesirables whom Robert Christenberry, the New York State Athletic Commissioner, has pledged himself to clean up. Some of them have criminal records, but to-day they are leaning over backwards in their attempts to woo respectability. True, my friend Ray Arcel was beaten up in 1953, but that was not directly connected with the fight game. American fight mobs to-day are not as tough as race-gangs who operated in London and Brighton half a century and less ago before the British Boxing Board of Control came into existence. Promoters wouldn't even spend the money for police or efficient stewards to keep order, and so many a night I saw the boys take the law into their own hands.

One wild scene stands out in my memory as though it happened but yesterday, when mob-law ruled and a race-gang swept down on an unsuspecting fight crowd like a swarm of locusts descending on a plantation stripping the onlookers of diamond rings, tie-pins, gold watches and thousands of pounds in bank-notes.

These were not characters with a Chicago background. They were just a tough, hungry bunch of bad boys from London's East End who, armed with razors, coshes and knuckle-dusters, had organised this raid—more daring and impudent than any I have known before or since.

The whole scene is as clear to me as though it were being re-acted on a television screen before my eyes. Draw up your chair and you will hardly believe your own eyes. It is a sweaty, sultry Saturday afternoon in July, 1909. The temperature is high in the nineties. We are gathered on the old Memorial Grounds in Canning Town, London, to see the third needle battle between Johnny Summers, the murderous-hitting British lightweight champion, and dapper Jimmy Britt, the great little scrapper from San Francisco, who had fought the best light-weights of them all—Battling Nelson, Joe Gans and Packey McFarland.

This is a bitter battle for Britt had gained a much disputed decision over the Englishman at Wonderland the previous year, and Summers had reversed this later over 20 rounds at the National Sporting Club. Feeling is high, and as we go into the ninth round the fair-headed Yorkshire fighter is getting on top. Britt's eyes are rolling. His face is the colour of putty as his strength is being sapped partly by the heat of the afternoon but more so by the terrible body blows that Summers is tossing at him.

The crowd are yelling. They can see Britt wilting. Then

16

suddenly he goes down. Glassy-eyed he struggles to one knee. Billy Tucker, who claimed to be the world champion ball-puncher, rushes from his corner with a soaked sponge, and showers Britt from head to foot as he kneels drunkenly. Summers, a fiery man at the best of times, is outraged at this American slick trick. The blood drains from his face. His eyes flash angrily, and he leaps towards the ropes to smack down Tucker, but is pulled back by the referee, Mr. Ted Humphries. Britt needed more than a sponge to clear his befuddled brain . . . 8 . . . 9 . . . out. It is a Summers' victory by a knockout. Then IT happens. It began innocently enough like a slap-happy crowd delighted at the Englishman's great win. But soon we realise a crisis is on us. Faces, happy a few seconds earlier, are now panic-stricken. Laughter fades away and for a few seconds there is a warning hush. Then a high pitched woman's scream sends a chill down my spine.

I am confused myself as the crowd begins to stampede and move towards the ringside where I am seated. Free fights are going on wherever I look. Some men are hysterical. Others are blaspheming. And all the time fists are flying. I am still too dumb-founded to move when suddenly a local boxer named Ted Moore who has already climbed into the ring leans over the ropes and calls out: "You'll be safer up here, Mr. Butler. I smell trouble."

There was trouble all right . . . plenty of it. From the outskirts of the large crowd an organised bunch of thugs advances, in a solid mass attack, planned with the skill of a modern Commando raid. There must be two to three hundred of the boys, robbing spectators with lightning speed. Watch-chains are ripped from waist-coats of indignant men. Race-glasses are snapped from straps by one swish of a razor and wallets are snatched from the surprised crowd mostly too afraid to protest. Even gold spectacles are grabbed from their owners' noses.

To resist is asking for trouble. One big fellow protests, but is immediately silenced by a cosh and as he rests there is given a most scientific and speedy going over. The little fellow with the rat-like face and ferret eyes who has slugged him even relieves his unconscious victim of his dental plate. This, after all, is a gold rush.

Freddy Welsh is standing there immaculately dressed. He looks flabbergasted as he thumbs his boater off his forehead to the back of his head, and then places both hands on his hips. But nobody touches Freddy. It may be that these mobsters in spite of being armed with coshes, do not wish to tackle the tough Pontypridd battler. Or perhaps it is because of their peculiar code that the race boys do not "give the business" to Welsh. Freddy is left quite unmolested.

About thirty or forty of us who have climbed inside the ring are left alone. I guess there is such a haul among ringside spectators that the robbers can't be bothered to make the extra effort of getting inside the ropes.

A party of rich American sportsmen who have come to support Jimmy Britt provide a rich haul, and three former champions and several famous jockeys are less fortunate than Freddy Welsh. They are stripped of several hundred pounds worth of notes, watches and diamonds.

One lucky fellow at the ringside is dapper Danny Maher. He gets a thorough going-over by one of the experts, but hasn't a bean on him. Danny, a wise-guy himself, has, with some friends, handed several thousand pounds in bank-notes to the safe-keeping of Ted Humphries, who has stuffed fivers, tenners, fifty and even hundred-pound notes inside his shirt and has refereed the big fight with them next to his skin! Later I am travelling home on a tram with Mr. Humphries and when we reach the "Kings and Keys" pub in Fleet Street we are naturally enough still talking about the amazing happenings of that afternoon. "Come here, Jimmy," laughs Ted, "I want to show you something." It was then I see with my own eyes several hundred Bank of England notes sticking to Humphries' body.

That was the scene on that hot July afternoon in 1909. Looking back I recall that, in spite of the happenings, there was a moment for smiles in which the famous Jolly Jumbo figured. Jolly Jumbo—his real name was William Ecclestone—was the ponderous sportsman who scaled close on forty stone and was a well-known character wherever boxing took place. He was acting as Britt's check timekeeper and wore on his wrist an ornate gold stop-watch.

Jolly had tried to climb up into the ring, but couldn't make it and his watch soon captured the attention of two of the gang. Jumbo was bowled over—all forty stone of him. One of the boys sat on his flabby chest, while the other struggled to wrench the huge watch from his fat wrists. All this time, Jumbo was going bluer in the face as he protested that it was a crying shame that he of all people should be subject to such an undignified position.

But the two mobsters showed little respect for Boxing's Fat Boy in spite of all the threats of what he would do to them when he climbed to his feet again. However, he won the day. Jumbo had wrists as thick as a young elephant's legs and an outsized strap of tough leather had been especially made to fit this valuable watch. The strap lashed to his wrist was so thick that no knife could cut through it!

Bob Scanlon, the coloured fighter, was seized and when they could not find any valuables on him, they stood him on his head and shook him until he rattled like castanets but only a few coppers fell out.

Alf Mitchell, the old knuckle fighter from Cardiff, was a hero that afternoon. He rescued one elderly sports-writer, Tom Dunning of *The Sportsman*, who was being set upon by a bunch of thugs. Alf went in with both fists swinging. He dropped four or five bewildered men and then, placing his hefty frame in front of the old scribe, led him to safety.

Although this raid frightened people away from open-air fights for months afterwards, the spectators were not the only losers. When Summers and Britt called to collect their purse they found the office door wide open. The cashier had departed.

Summers quickly caught up with one of the partners in the pro-motion and with backing from tough local supporters refused to leave the ground until he was paid something in hard cash.

19

Jimmy Britt was less fortunate. Some weeks later I met him in the Strand, and he told me the most he had been able to collect in full settlement was £75.

Britt never fought again. When Packey McFarland came to England to fight Freddy Welsh at the N.S.C., Jimmy came along and stayed at McFarland's camp at Jack Straw's Castle on Hampstead Heath. Later he joined up with the Australian promoter, Hugh D. McIntosh, who put on big-time boxing at Olympia. The American, who could rattle off any quotation from Shakespeare, had a great ambition to become an actor. He appeared on the stage of the Tivoli and Oxford Music Halls in a monologue turn, and later secured a contract for an American vaudeville tour, but, like the majority of pugilists, Jimmy never really put himself across the footlights. He belonged beneath the arc-lights of the ring.

Summers, blond and square of jaw, lacked the polish and ambition of Britt, but he was a born fighter and was the hardest-hitting lightweight I ever saw . . . a bigger puncher than Eric Boon. Johnny was an exponent of the dying art of straight-hitting. He is one of the few fighters I watched land a knockout with a straight left.

There was another reason why I shall never forget the afternoon of the Summers-Britt grand slam. I was booked to referee some of the preliminary bouts, and had already taken up my position in the official chair when another boxing writer, a Scotsman, Bob Wilson, pleaded with me to let him take over. Having refereed scores of big fights, the honour and glory didn't mean much to me, so I readily climbed down.

Two local boys came into the ring, and soon we had a needle atmosphere with spectators from **all** sides of the ring joining in, and the referee came in for abuse from both **factions**. When he had given his decision, friends of the loser took exception. One of them hurried to the ringside, and took a running kick at the base of Wilson's spine. It was a cowardly act, and I felt sick as I heard an awful crack, thinking Bob's back must have been broken, but it was the thug who suffered. He let out a sharp yell, and grabbed his foot in pain.

Bob Wilson walked off unhurt. It was then I remembered he had spinal trouble and that his back was encased in a steel waistcoat!

The scene I have described was extraordinary, but they were altogether tough days forty and fifty years ago, and referees had to be fearless. Frequently, the officials were targets for the betting boys whose favourite ammunition was the bomb shaped soda-water bottle with glass marble lodged in the neck.

Boxing was without a ruling body, the sport being un-officially but efficiently controlled by the three sporting news-papers who appointed the officials. Many times when acting as time-keeper or referee I had to duck these "bombs." I smile a little when I recall the afternoon the late J. T. Hulls was referee and I the time-keeper at Bow when Fred Drummond of Blackfriars and Harry Shearing of Walthamstow were in action. Hull's decision upset one of the gangs and they descended on the ringside. "Quick, Jimmy" shouted J. T., "if you can't run—now's the time to learn unless you want your throat slit."

I didn't even stop to consider that the boys were after the referee and not the timekeeper. My heart was thumping as we both ran out of the arena with four thugs in pursuit. We were only saved by the presence of a passing bus which was as welcome as a raft to a drowning man.

The mob boys didn't care two hoots where they struck. On one hot afternoon in July, 1921, Pete Herman, the world bantamweight champion, was weighing in for his bout with Jim Higgins, the Scot who had won outright a Lonsdale Belt in 11 months, at the National Sporting Club. The contest was due to take place that night in the Club's new headquarters at Holland Park Rink, but the weigh-in ceremony was held in the Covent Garden premises. Members of one of England's most notorious race-gangs crashed in through the stage-door. As Higgins climbed on the scales there was the usual hush as specators listened for the announcement of the weights. Suddenly a blood-curdling scream pierced the theatre. The leader of the gang had slashed the face of a thug belonging to a rival gang.

Billy Plimmer, the clever Birmingham bantamweight who won the British title, took up refereeing and made his début at the misnamed Wonderland in Whitechapel. Officials used to sit on the stage some twenty or thirty rows from the ring. Billy got through the preliminaries without trouble but upset the boys with his verdict for the top-liner. Billy, too, had to run for his life. Even so his thigh was grazed with a pocket-knife as he escaped through the door.

I met Billy later in the evening and he was fuming. He had returned to the Wonderland to collect his fees from Harry Jacobs, the astute and hard-boiled manager and matchmaker. "How much do you think the so-and-so paid me?" growled Plimmer, and before I could venture a guess, he snapped, "Ten dirty silver shillings, and to think the boys nearly operated on me!"

Ted Humphries was the most fearless of all the referees I knew. A powerfully built man with a barrel chest—his real name was Teddy Coffin. He had played League football and could take care of himself with his own fists.

I was acting as timekeeper at the old King's Hall, near the Elephant and Castle, the night he disqualified Young Nipper of Bermondsey in an early round. The local crowd were furious and screamed encouragement when one of Nipper's friends picked up the water-bottle to attack the referee. Humphries grabbed the man with his ham-like hands, snatched the bottle off him and stood in the middle of the ring swinging it like a baseball bat inviting anybody in the hall to come and get him.

Professor Joe Smith, the matchmaker, afraid of trouble, implored me to take over the referee's chair for the rest of the bouts, but Humphries retorted: "Nobody is going to sit in this chair tonight but myself. Those thugs out there are not going to intimidate me." And there he remained to the end of the show with the water-bottle within easy reach in case anybody had other ideas.

CHAPTER II

JACK JOHNSON—GREATEST OF 'EM ALL

THE GREATEST HEAVYWEIGHT of the last half century was Jack Johnson. The coloured giant from Texas possessed the brute strength of the gorilla, yet moved with the smooth stealth of the panther, and took into the ring a defensive skill that was out of this world. He had a smarter fighting brain than any pugilist I have known, including Gene Tunney.

No other king of the ring lived such a life of contradictions. He was poor, he was rich, idolised and hated. He was sentenced to a year in the penitentiary, and yet escaped arrest and lived like a king in Europe, Mexico, South America and Cuba—living in a fool's paradise for a number of years before finally returning to pay his debt to society by serving his prison sentence.

Johnson became arrogant and drunk with his own physical achievements. He sneered at his white brethren and boasted of his many conquests of those white women infatuated by this Black Prince. I am not excusing Lil' Arthur, as he liked to refer to himself, for his sins which were many, but before you judge him remember he had been born at Galveston, Texas, at a period when there were insurmountable prejudices against the Negro in America. He became the first coloured man to win the world's heavyweight title. He had been down-trodden in his youth by the white man, who had kicked his black behind and slapped his kinky head.

He approached adolescence with good cause to dislike his superior brother, and as he grew and grew into a tall and muscular giant he became more and more conscious of his physical powers and vowed one day he would be in the position

23

to physically dominate any human in the world. And then he would show the white boss just where to get off.

Johnson controlled this bitterness until finally he had caught up with and dethroned Tommy Burns to become heavyweight champion of the world. Then all the suppressed hatred poured forth from his soul. Once he had let go he lost all self-control and stoked up the existing hatred against him.

Yet he was a remarkable fellow. Although born in modest surroundings, he spoke French, German and Spanish fluently. He ran his own night clubs in Chicago, packed music-halls for his stage appearances, stopped traffic in every capital of Europe he visited, fought and killed three bulls in Barcelona on his first public appearance. So you see Lil' Arthur was not just a man of muscle and brawn.

Johnson was never extended in the 7 years he held the heavyweight title. Not even at the age of 37 when he lost his crown to Jess Willard, the 18-stone cowboy from Pottawatomie County, Kansas, at Havana, Cuba, in 1915. He confessed to me years after in New York that he had sold his crown for a "bag of gold" plus the advice of white folk that once he had lost his title he would be allowed to return to the United States a free man.

Johnson simply toyed with Tommy Burns, at Rushcutters Bay, Sydney, in 1908. True, the outstanding middleweight of them all, Stanley Ketchell, caught him off guard and dropped him in the 12th round at Colma, California, in 1909, but the 6 ft. Negro got up and immediately knocked Ketchell unconscious with a right uppercut.

Johnson, I believe, would have beaten John L. Sullivan, Gentleman Jim Corbett, Bob Fitzsimmons and Jim Jeffries at their best. He knocked out Ruby Bob in two rounds when old Fitz was near the end of the road. And Jeffries, at the age of 35, was unable to regain the heavyweight title from Lil' Arthur.

The pity of it all was that Johnson never had the balance to help himself or his race. Never before had a coloured boy in America had a wish come true bringing him overnight power, wealth, the friendship of rulers and the adoration of attractive white women. In spite of all the prejudice against the coloured folk at that time, Johnson could have become an ambassador of his people. He could have won the respect and friendship of white folk . . . just as a less educated and less intelligent Joe Louis did nearly 30 years later.

It was Sam Langford who dropped the first hint in Britain about the might of Johnson. The remarkable Boston Tar Baby had come to the N.S.C. in 1907 to knock Tiger Smith, the Welsh "southpaw," bow-legged in four rounds. So impressed were members by the Boston Tar Baby's performance that one of them called for "Three cheers for Sam Langford, the real heavyweight champion of the world." (Tommy Burns held the title at the time.) But the modest Langford interrupted, "Say, boss, that's not me. There's a big smoke back home called Jack Johnson who is unbeatable. He licked me in Massachusetts last year and he's improving every month."

I didn't meet Johnson until some months later in 1908 when he arrived in London almost broke, having crossed the Atlantic by a third class passage. He was still trying to catch up with Tommy Burns for a world title match. Tall, slim and panther-like in his movement, he was neatly but cheaply dressed, quiet in manner and full of personality. I often visited him at a hotel in Adelphi Terrace behind the old Tivoli music-hall in London's Strand. Many literary personalities lived on the Terrace, notably George Bernard Shaw.

At this time, Johnson had all his bitterness completely under control. A Colonel Kelly, who lived in the hotel and stood two inches above Johnson, was a Negro-hater, and resented the coloured giant's intrusion in the hotel. On numerous occasions after drinking bouts, he stupidly challenged Johnson to come outside and fight. I once heard the aggressive and huge Kelly insult Johnson to such an extent that I would gladly have given testimony for the Negro had he flattened the ill-mannered Colonel on the spot. "You niggers," sneered Kelly, "are all yellow-livered. You don't like being hit in the belly."

Johnson must have flushed beneath his black skin, but he never raised his voice. Instead he smiled, and replied "You're right, Colonel, but you know any white fellows who like being hit in the same place?"

Johnson had only two so-called fights in England, both at the Cosmopolitan Club at Plymouth. In June he tackled Al McNamara and won in 4 rounds and in July he knocked out Ben Taylor, known as the Woolwich Infant, in 8 rounds. This was five months before he was to win the title from Burns and he was only raising funds for his boat-fare to Australia. He also took part in music hall engagements here to raise more cash. Johnson's arrogant attitude whether inside or outside the ring made him enemies. Although he carried a big punch, Johnson preferred cat-and-mouse tactics. He could have put many of his victims out of their misery, but enjoyed goading them with his jibes.

He had chased Tommy Burns across America, through Europe and on to Australia. So sure was he of success that he accepted £1,538 as his share while Burns collected £6,212. He even agreed that Hugh D. McIntosh, who was the promoter and a friend of Burns, could act as referee. Throughout the 14 rounds before the police intervened Johnson toyed with the world champion. As he drew blood from Tommy's puffed lips he would drawl: "How do you like this one, Tommy?" and as he sunk left and right hooks into Burns' body, Tommy would grunt and Johnson flashed his golden teeth and sneered: "Who has got the yellow streak now?"

He was the same cocky goader when he fought Jim Jeffries at Reno, Nevada, on July 4, 1910. Jeffries had been retired undefeated champion six years, but so desperate had become the search for a White Hope that Old Jim was finally persuaded to come back against Johnson.

Pompadour Jim Corbett, victor over the mighty John L. Sullivan, was engaged to advise Jeffries. Johnson merely teased Jeffries, and enjoyed himself baiting Corbett. As he punished the old champion, who had no right to be in the same

26

ring, Jack would turn a head to Gentleman Jim and sneer: "Guess you couldn't take what I'm handing out to Jeff" and, "Who told you that you were a great champion?"

Outside the ring he carried on his own business with equal arrogance. He had promised the late "Peggy" Bettinson, boss of the old National Sporting Club, that should he become world champion he would defend his title in the club against Sam Langford. On the strength of this, "Peggy" had advanced some cash towards Lil' Arthur's fare to Australia.

Once Johnson had the title he wasn't interested in the National Sporting Club. Bettinson, himself a martinet, was so angry that he persuaded the club committee to ban all coloured fighters from the club. This rule was modified when the Boxing Board of Control was founded in 1929, but still any fighter born in Great Britain with coloured blood was barred from boxing for a British title. It is only since the end of the last war that coloured boys like Dick and Randy Turpin have been able to fight for the championships of the country they were born in. They can blame Johnson and the dictatorial "Peggy" Bettinson for this unjust rule.

As world champion, Johnson was hated in his own country. His enemies grew almost daily as he strutted on Broadway and lived like a king in Chicago. He loved the company of white women, marrying three times and enjoying a fistful of white show-girls. His loose and dangerous living finally caught up with him in America when he became associated with a young girl from Minnesota who was attending a Chicago school. Women he had loved and scorned were called as witnesses against him and he was charged for violating the Mann act and sentenced to one year and a day imprisonment.

While on bail, Johnson cleverly organised an escape to Canada and from there he sailed for Europe. He was a fugitive from his own country, but still a king abroad, and attracted immense crowds in every capital he visited.

The day he drove down Fleet Street, police diverted cars and buses on to the Thames Embankment as thousands of men and women and children caused a congestion in their attempt to get a glimpse of the fabulous Negro. A coloured man in the streets of London was an unusual sight in these days.

I had squeezed into the doorway of a tailor's shop facing St. Bride's Church, and joined in the conversation of two Americans in ten-gallon hats. "We're sure amazed by the homage you British are showing this big shine," they told me, "the moment he steps on United States territory he's under arrest."

I asked these cowboy-like fellows if they knew a cousin of mine, Big Dick Butler, a New York Assemblyman and himself a character. They sure did, and introduced themselves. They were Tex Rickard, the greatest promoter of them all, and his right-hand man Jim Coffroth.

It was the same wherever Johnson went throughout Europe. He hit the headlines in Paris, Vienna, Brussels, Berlin and Moscow. It was the glamour of all this that caused Johnson to forget he was a fugitive from justice.

Johnson didn't seem to be able to avoid controversy—in fact, he loved the limelight and took the attitude that bad publicity was better than no publicity. James White, the financier who was to commit suicide, was in big money at this period and tried to match Johnson with Bombardier Billy Wells.

Wells would have stood little chance against Johnson, but the match never developed anyway because a South London clergyman condemned the match and eventually an injunction was granted and the case was heard at Bow Street. Thousands crowded the streets, and I was subpœnaed as a witness, but was not called to give evidence.

Johnson showed his cuteness when a constable began quoting statements about boxing rules. Lil' Arthur flashed his teeth and said: "Sure, you're right, officer. You are reading from a record under the ledge of the desk."

In spite of his playboy antics and careless living, Johnson was too good for all opposition in Europe. In Paris he defended his title against Jim Johnson. The referee called it a draw after Lil'

Arthur had declared he had broken his arm. He then out-pointed Frank Moran, the Pittsburgh dentist, whose right hand punch was known as the "Mary Ann."

Johnson was running out of opponents and he was living at such a pace that he was spending his cash quicker than he could earn it. So he was impressed when some former white associates arrived from America with a proposition for him to defend his crown against Jess Willard.

Johnson said afterwards he was told he could make a nice little bit on the side by losing, and that once he had ceased to hold the world title the hatred that was still increasing in his own country would simmer down and that, minus the champion-ship, he would stand a good chance of obtaining a pardon from his own country and would then be able to return to America a free man again and could then engage in a prosperous occupation and make new friends.

Originally, it was intended to stage the fight in Juarez, Mexico, and Pancho Villa, the revolutionary bandit leader who then controlled northern Mexico, was supposed to be interested in staging the bout.

Johnson, with a certain amount of advanced cash, sailed for South America in 1914 and then on to Barbados in the West Indies and then to Havana, Cuba. Lil' Arthur, hearing rumours that President Carranza of Mexico intended to capture the world heavyweight champion if he attempted to box for the bandit leader, refused to go to Mexico and so Frazee and Webber, amusement promoters, who were helping to back the fight decided to put it on in Havana.

Well, it is history what happened on a blazing afternoon. Johnson after having the better of the early fight finally took the count in the 26th round. There is a famous picture of the knockout. Willard is standing with hands flopping at his sides, and the Negro is stretched out, his right forearm up to his eyes as though protecting them from the glaring sunshine. Many insist Johnson is grinning as he takes the count.

I questioned Johnson when I met him in New York early in

1946. Lil' Arthur was by then an old man and had mellowed with the years, but he insisted that he sold his title that night.

"Sure, it was a frame-up," Johnson told me, "A frame-up for freedom. I was short of cash and I was all mixed up. I wanted to return to my own country. Frazee and Webber assured me they had fixed all the preliminaries for my freedom provided I lost to Willard.

"In addition to a sum of money to be paid to my wife at the ringside, I was to have the exclusive rights of the film of the fight which I could take on exhibition to Europe and South America.

"I received my percentage due to me before the fight, but the additional percentage promised me to lose was paid near the end of the fight. It was only after my wife gave me a pre-arranged signal that I decided to take the count. She was paid the money in 500 dollar bills."

Johnson insisted this story was true. I am never quite sure whether he was telling the truth or whether in late years he tried to recapture some of the past superiority of the white fighters by convincing himself that he could have beaten Willard in 1915. After all he was then 38 and his way of living must have taken a toll on him.

But Lil' Arthur was particularly bitter as he related the story because he said the men behind the scenes did everything to get out of their part of the bargain. They had done nothing towards getting him pardoned and that he had to return to London. The film of the fight eventually arrived, but was blank. Then the real films turned up and Johnson had to take matters into his own hands to come by them.

Johnson staged a come-back in Spain against moderate opposition and engaged in bull-fighting. When he hung up his gloves in 1926 he had little left of the fortune he had earned with his fists.

Among his weaknesses was the passion to drive a motor-car as fast as it would go. He had four almost miraculous escapes in 1925 when he turned over cars at break-neck speed smashing them to smithereens.

But you can't laugh death in the face forever. I was still in America after my chat with Johnson in June 1946, when I picked up a New York newspaper to read that Lil' Arthur had taken his last drive—this time into the way beyond. The then 68 year old Negro was speeding when he lost control of a large automobile and crashed at Franklington City, North Carolina. This time it was a Negro passenger who escaped with his life. But Lil' Arthur died some hours later at St. Agnes Hospital. And so the curtain fell on the career of the most fabulous and greatest pugilist of our time.

CHAPTER III

PEERLESS JIM

IT WAS A bleak February day 'way back in 1925 when the funeral dragged morbidly along the packed streets of Cardiff. Even the stranger to that City knew this was not just another death march through the Welsh capital. More than 100,000 people jammed the pavements—their heads bare, their eyes downcast. Traffic became chaotic, and for a few minutes life in the main streets of Cardiff stood still as the procession— more than a mile long—passed.

And what a mixed gathering it was. There were little children each with a wreath clasped nervously in both hands. And there were unusual looking men with square shoulders, flattened noses and battered ears, who might have stepped out of a Damon Runyon book. Their very appearance suggested they were tough. Yet this day they marched in public unashamed as a tear or two slid down a rough cheek like drips from a burning candle.

Old women with skins as wrinkled as dried prunes hobbled along dabbing tear-sore eyes with grubby handkerchiefs. And coloured folk from the Tiger Bay area strolled to stare curiously as Cardiff paid its last respects to a man who had been idolised and loved by young and old. It was the last journey home for Jim Driscoll . . . Peerless Jim.

No other pugilist before or since has been mourned so greatly by his fellow men and women. Great scrappers like Owen Moran, Johnny Basham, Tiger Smith and many others followed the coffin.

Boxing lost more than a friend and a good fellow when Jim Driscoll was snatched from the life he enjoyed so much when

JAMES BUTLER

JACK DEMPSEY—THE MANASSA MAULER

only 45. Something died with him that has never quite been replaced—and never will. I could almost say the straight left passed from British boxing with Driscoll. This punch, once admired by foreign pugilists all over the world lingers on in England but even our amateurs are forsaking it now because judges and referees in foreign competition no longer appreciate its use for scoring points. I blame the modern boxers for this state, because the straight left has developed into a slap—just like an interior decorator slapping whitewash on to a ceiling. Those of you not old enough to have seen Driscoll perform haven't really seen the straight left as it should be. Peerless Jim didn't just stick his left glove out hoping to score a few points. He closed his fist and then proceeded to split open eyebrows and flatten noses, leaving his opponents with heads so dizzy that they were softened up for his right cross.

As a scientific boxer Driscoll was incomparable. Everything he did in the ring was stamped with class. He was the perfect, polished stylist who with the slightest glance of his head could cause opponents on the attack to stumble, reel, and sometimes hurtle into the ropes as helpless as drunken sailors. He never wasted a punch, nor an ounce of energy, but because he didn't indulge in the two-fisted whirlwind style of successful American battlers, don't get the impression that Driscoll was just a pretty boxer and a dancing master to be admired. Peerless Jim was Merciless Jim in the ring, and packed a deadly punch in either hand. He was born with the gift of being able to time his punches quite naturally. That was one of the secrets of his success. And the fact that he earned the title of "Peerless" at a time when Britain boasted of so many outstanding fighters—men like Freddy Welsh from Pontypridd, Tom Thomas, the Welsh farmer, and Digger Stanley, the caravan dweller, to name but a few—emphasises his greatness.

Although born at Cardiff, Driscoll had a large drop of Irish blood flowing through his veins, and had a quick fighting temper and a tongue that could lash an opponent with as much fury as could his fists. Yet he schooled himself not to lose his head inside the ring . . . although he was frequently involved in heated arguments outside. Only once did I see Jim rattled in a fight and that was in the bitter battle with Freddy Welsh at Cardiff . . . a bout that developed into a rough-house, and ended with Driscoll being disqualified in the 10th round for butting.

Jim was just about the most handsome pugilist the ring has known. In his early days his hair was black as coal and curly. He had laughing blue eyes, and a perfectly chiselled Greek profile. My first memory of this striking Celt was at the National Sporting Club forty-six years ago when he made a tremendous impression on the members and a dozen newspaper critics who sat on the stage by punching Jack Roberts of Drury Lane into submission in seven rounds. Roberts was a typical pugilist of the old school, but the young Cardiff boxer jabbed his head almost off his shoulders, and drew so much blood that Roberts looked more like a Red Indian when he was knocked out.

Driscoll twice defeated Joe Bowker of Salford who had won the British bantam title from Pedlar Palmer, and the world crown from Frankie Neil of America. Bowker was himself a wonderful boxer but he never had a chance with Driscoll who beat him in fifteen rounds and later in seventeen rounds. In the second fight Bowker did a great deal of holding, and I can't say I blamed him, because that tantalising left hand was never out of his face. Bowker's only hope was to get close in and batter away at Driscoll's stomach which all through his life was Jim's only weak spot.

But Driscoll's temper was rising, and finally his eyes flashed and he spat out "Let go! Who do you think you are— Hackenschmidt?" Jim's tongue often had him in trouble. After he had defeated Charley Griffin, a tough Australian, his opponent, unsatisfied with the decision, asked for a return match. As was the custom at the old National Sporting Club, the contestants of any big fight gathered in the Strangers' Room of the club next day to sip champagne. Griffin questioned the decision again, and Jim not only abused the Australian with his tongue, but was ready to start a fight on the spot.

And when Bombardier Billy Wells was knocked out in jig-time by Georges Carpentier in 1913, Driscoll was so incensed at the poor showing by Wells that he rushed to the ringside and hot-headedly sneered at the Bombardier and accused him of cowardice. Poor Wells, already humiliated by the lighter Frenchman, shook his head sadly and mumbled: "Please don't talk like that Jim." One of the club members rightly took exception to Driscoll's behaviour and began pushing the Cardiff boxer from the ringside. Driscoll's eyes were hot, his fists were clenched, but he controlled himself, realising he had made a fool of himself. Later he apologised to Wells, and they remained good friends till Driscoll's death.

I have told you how that almost uncontrollable temper played such a big part in Driscoll's life, but in spite of his waspish tongue, Jim was kind and generous. He fought as a featherweight, but stepped up into the heavyweight class when it came to his heart. He was, in fact, a fool to himself when it came to cash. Driscoll was horse-racing crazy. Not only did he lose most of his money that way, but on the best-known race tracks he was reckoned to be an "easy touch" for the professional tappers.

And on his frequent visits to the National Sporting Club either as a contestant or a spectator he had at least one regular client. An old boxer whom Driscoll had annihilated some years earlier. The poor fellow would wait outside, his battered face beneath an old cap, always on the look-out for Driscoll with the request for a half a sovereign. Peerless Jim never once refused.

Following his wonderful "No Decision" display against the world featherweight champion, Abe Attell, when most New York boxing writers agreed Driscoll had outboxed Attell, he was offered big money for those days to stay on in America. But Jim had promised to box an exhibition at the annual tournament for the poor Cardiff children of Nazareth House, and because Driscoll's word was his bond, turned down

35

thousands of dollars in order to keep faith with these boys and girls. It was the children of Nazareth House who later followed the coffin of their friend who had done so much to help them.

Driscoll had first gone to America in 1908 after having beaten Harry Mansfield—the only fighter to have gained a decision over him up to this time. He boxed in the States under the management of an old friend of mine, the late Charley Harvey. Harvey, who specialised in handling English boxers, had told America that Driscoll was the greatest featherweight ever, but when Driscoll arrived at the New York docks wearing a cap, and carrying a small-sized grip, Harvey had had to dash off to California, and he sent Jimmy Johnston to meet Driscoll. Johnston thought Charley had made his biggest-ever mistake when Driscoll stripped at Jack Cooper's gymnasium. All the boxing writers were there to see this "unveiling" of Peerless Jim. They expected to see a modern Hercules. And what did they see? . . . A skinny fellow with a long neck and deep depressions about the upper chest which suggested weak lungs. And on top of this Driscoll coughed badly. But they forgot all about his physical appearance when he boxed first with Jack Doyle, a tough middleweight, and then with Johnston himself who had been a fair scrapper around the time of Terry McGovern. Johnston didn't believe it possible. He couldn't lay a glove on the Cardiff Wizard, and every time this scraggy British boy hit him he thought the roof had caved in.

Driscoll was never beaten in America, although most of his fights were "No Decision" affairs, but had a decision been given the night he boxed Attell, Driscoll must have become undisputed world featherweight champion.

A year after returning from America, Jim was matched with Seaman Hayes of Hoxton for the first Lonsdale featherweight Belt. Hayes was a sturdy fellow, but no match for Driscoll, and was outclassed in six rounds.

Two months later the Cardiff champion was defending his newly won title against a great featherweight from North Shields, Frank Spike Robson. This proved a sensational bout. Driscoll had not trained and was well below his best and was, in fact, lucky to retain his title. Robson, who had come in the ring with his hair completely shaved off just to outdo his trainer who was almost bald, was a relentless two-handed fighter, and succeeded in splitting a cut above Driscoll's right eye which was almost closed after four rounds. As the bell sounded for the fifth, Robson came tearing out like a mad bull before the champion had left his corner and aimed a wild right swing. In spite of his injury Driscoll moved his head with that uncanny accuracy, and Robson floundered forward, and crashed his head on the edge of the stool which had not been removed quickly enough. When he rose blood was gushing down his face, half blinding him. In spite of this the game Robson carried on for another ten rounds before Driscoll knocked him out. By that time he was so badly beaten that he was carried to his dressing room where he remained unconscious for nearly an hour.

A little over a year ago Randy Turpin had his world title taken from him while still standing on his feet, and unmarked whereas his opponent Robinson was bleeding from a terrible gash. Certainly no present-day referee in the world would have allowed Spike Robson to have continued. But at this time the referee seldom left his chair outside the ring, and hardly ever examined a boxer's injury.

After this bout Driscoll slipped back to America for a "No Decision" contest with Pal Moore—not the same opponent who fought Jimmy Wilde twice—in Philadelphia. He returned to take part in the bitterest battle of his career with Freddy Welsh, whose correct name was Fred Hall Thomas. This grim struggle took place at the old Westgate Street Rink in Cardiff five days before Christmas of 1910. It captured the imagination of Wales. The Irish population of Cardiff was behind Driscoll, the rest rooted 100% for Welsh, who although born at Pontypridd, had begun his fighting in Philadelphia.

Welsh and Driscoll had never liked each other. As soon as Freddy ducked under the ropes he cast a contemptuous glance at his lighter opponent. It was deliberate tactics to rouse the

Driscoll temper, because Welsh, a strong two-fisted American-styled battler, realised he could not match the featherweight for skill, but in a rough-house scrap Welsh had few masters.

For four rounds it was all Driscoll. He gave the Pontypridd battler a lesson with his left hand, but Welsh was determined to get inside, and when he succeeded he opened up a vicious kidney attack which he learned in America where this type of fighting is not illegal. Driscoll's supporters hooted angrily, and Jim appealed to the referee, "Peggy" Bettinson, but no action was taken. Three rounds later Driscoll carried an angry red patch round both kidneys, and Welsh had certainly succeeded in rattling the featherweight champion, who was trying to fight back instead of continuing his clever boxing. Welsh, seeing that the referee was not objecting and that Jim was disturbed, kept up this attack, and also roused Driscoll's ire further by bringing up his head sharply in the clinches.

Peerless Jim completely lost his head. He allowed Welsh to dictate the way the fight should be fought. It was the only time I saw Driscoll not in control of himself in the ring, and the only time I ever saw him stoop to foul tactics. So bitter was the hatred by the tenth round that the finest boxer this country has ever produced was rushing in red-eyed like a man gone berserk. Science, ringcraft, defence—these things were forgotten. There was but one idea in the Cardiff boxer's mind and that was to hammer and smash this sneering opponent to the canvas.

It was now a street-corner fight, and not a pretty sight to watch, both men butting whenever the opportunity came. "Peggy" Bettinson was to blame. He had allowed Welsh to get away with "murder" and the struggle had got out of his grip now. They were going at each other like wildcats when Driscoll, his blue eyes now blazing, smashed lefts and rights to Welsh's ribs. Freddy always an "ivy" fighter clung to Driscoll, and kept up his kidney attacks. The infuriated Driscoll pulled his head back and, with a sickening thud, butted Welsh under the chin, and flung him half-way across the ring.

Freddy staggered and Driscoll, completely mad with temper

now, went in for the kill, but the referee was roused at last, and climbed into the ring and dragged the crazy pair of combatants apart. He motioned Driscoll back to his corner, and awarded the decision to Welsh. But that was only a start. A more bitter fight than ever was now raging. "Badger" Brian, in Driscoll's corner, rushed across to Boyo Driscoll, who was seconding Welsh, and they punched each other furiously. This was the signal, and soon the excited supporters of the two boxers were throwing punches at the first person who got in their way. It was broken up by the intervention of some sturdy Cardiff constables, but even they had a job to get Boyo Driscoll and Badger Brian apart. Still breathing lurid threats they agreed to fight it out in the ring at the first opportunity. They did this very thing, a few weeks later, but the bitterness had died, and the official contest brought yawns with the spontaneous and unofficial ringside bout.

"Peggy" Bettinson did not get off entirely. As soon as he had disqualified Driscoll, an angry supporter of Jim's stole his sable-lined overcoat which he had left over his chair. It was, however, insured.

This was the only time in Driscoll's brilliant career he had resorted to questionable tactics. He was heart-broken when I spoke to him in the dressing room: "Don't—tell me, Jimmy" he stammered, "I know I lost my head, and that's unforgivable for a fighter, but heaven knows I was provoked!"

Driscoll did everything to get Welsh back in the ring, but that was not to be. Five weeks later he knocked out Spike Robson in seven rounds to make the Lonsdale Belt his own property. Driscoll had only two fights in the next two years. He knocked out Jean Poesy and fought a 20 round draw with his old rival Owen Moran.

During the 1914-18 war, he was a R.S.M. on the Army Gymnastic Staff along with other champions like Johnny Basham, Jimmy Wilde, Pat O'Keefe, Dick Smith and Bombardier Billy Wells, who were sergeants.

In 1919, he beat Pedlar Palmer in 4 rounds. He was now

nearly forty and the jet black hair was tipped with grey. His face was lined, much of the old snap had gone, and he was only a shadow of the great Jim Driscoll we had known. Yet in spite of this I watched him box 20 brilliant rounds against Francis Rossi, of Pontypridd. 11,000 spectators paying £1,100 filled the corrugated-roofed hall of The Pavilion, Mountain Ash. Driscoll well won the decision, but old Dan Whelligan of Birkenhead declared a draw, and the crowds threw coppers into the ring. Driscoll had mellowed. Later he smiled at Whelligan who was embarrassed by the remarks his friends were making, and said: "Never mind, Dan. I would never question your honesty, but I just thought I won."

Driscoll's next fight was his last. And it was one of the most touching endings to a great champion's career.

His health was already deteriorating. His chest was beginning to trouble him, and he was having much pain in his stomach, but he wouldn't admit this to anybody, and when "Peggy" Bettinson offered him a 20 round battle with the great Charles Ledoux, a Parisian pastry-cook, Jim agreed.

His friends—myself included—could see the red light and pleaded with him to demand a fifteen round contest, but Jim replied: "I verbally agreed to 20 rounds, and I never go back on my word."

And so for 15 rounds, Driscoll a few months short of his fortieth birthday toyed with his stronger opponent who was twelve years younger. So much so that when a bookmaker in "Tattersalls" offered 33 to 1 on Driscoll there were not any takers.

Had the betting boys known what I knew that Jim had spent four days in bed before the fight they would have grabbed such odds. In spite of his physical deterioration, Driscoll had never boxed better. He was the supreme artist, and Ledoux, a great battler, was made to look a novice. But Jim's health and age were a bigger enemy than Ledoux, and the sixteenth round began with Jim so far ahead on points that the referee might well have stopped the bout because Ledoux had been outclassed.

But his legs were tired, and it was an effort for him to raise both hands. Ledoux and his foxy manager Francois Descamps knew this, and the little pastry-cook went in. A wicked body punch sent Driscoll the colour of a poor sailor in the Bay of Biscay, and Badger O'Brien, knowing that Jim Driscoll would never fight again, let out a pathetic groan and tossed in the towel to save the Peerless One the indignity of being knocked out.

Driscoll slipped to his dressing room realising for the first time in his life that skill alone was not sufficient. Ill health had licked him. Some club members were near tears, and they did not forget the greatness of Driscoll. The Club committee called an immediate meeting, and within half an hour a Testimonial Fund was launched for Peerless Jim and £1,500 raised that night. With various tournaments a total of £5,000 was subscribed for the finest boxer this country has produced.

Jim Driscoll, Prince of Sportsmen, King of the Ring, died five years later. He left neither a photo of himself in fighting pose, nor his Lonsdale Belt. Just a small cup with an appreciation roughly scratched on the bowl—"from the boys of Boulogne Garrison." This he promised me a week before he died. His widow handed the cup to Jimmy Wilde who brought it to London, and to-day it is perhaps the least valuable of my many trophies, but for me it is my most precious sporting treasure.

The Lonsdale belt, however, came into the possession of Driscoll's first cousin, Jim Ocker Burns, the old Cardiff and Welsh Rugby international who is "Mine Host" at the Royal Hotel, Newport Road, Cardiff, where the trophy is on show.

CHAPTER IV

THE MANASSA MAULER AND PROFESSOR GENE

ALTHOUGH NEARLY FORTY years have passed since the fabulous Jack Johnson faded from the fistic horizon, only three great heavyweights have ascended the throne in those four decades ... Dempsey, Tunney and Louis. There have been plenty of giants parading—and some of them masquerading—but none of them, apart from the three I have named, even get a rating from me. Some have missed greatness by inches or by accident . . . like Max Baer, who could hit harder than any living man since Dempsey, but whose sense of humour outstripped his ring sense. Maxie preferred to crack a joke or a magnum of champagne rather than his opponents, and so goes down in boxing history not as a King of the Ring but as the Prince of Playboys.

How do I rate Dempsey, Tunney and Louis? Dempsey is placed above Tunney, because without Dempsey there never would have been a Tunney. Gene's fame and fortune can be pin-pointed to his two 10 round victories over a Dempsey who had been softened by the glamorous living that a few million dollars must inevitably bring. I doubt if Tunney would have been able to hold off the young, terrible, and hungry mauler from Manassa. When Tunney defeated him, Dempsey had mellowed and deteriorated like a jungle king who had spent years under the captivity of a cage. Set such a lion loose again and it would be easy prey for younger and fiercer rivals. That's how Tunney beat Dempsey. He waited his time watching the old champ deteriorating, and preparing for the day when he would be ready for the kill. For such patience and successful calculation, Tunney goes down as the brainiest and most unusual of all pugilists.

42

Louis, like Dempsey, gained immortal fame through sheer ability . . . not in two fights but over a fifteen years' trial. But for the last war, he would have been a more sensational champion and a richer man than he is to-day. Who would have survived between Dempsey and Louis at their best? A difficult choice to make, but pressed for an opinion, I would pick the Manassa Mauler.

I shall never forget Dempsey as first I saw him. Never before or since has a man been so suitably fitted for the role of world heavyweight champion. The perfect prize-fighter. Tough and rugged as though Nature herself had chiselled his physique and profile from granite. There he stood with black curly hair and blue chin. His dark eyes could flash from laughter to terrifying hatred in a split second.

A giant and a killer, yes. Yet more physically perfect than an ordinary giant, for he had the slender waist of a dancer and the legs of an athlete which accounted for his deceptive weight— he scaled only around 13st. 4 lb. at his best—and for his surprising speed inside the ring.

As important as these physical assets was the Dempsey outlook. He never regarded the ring as anything but a jungle which suited the brutal streak that was part of the Dempsey make-up. To survive and rule in this jungle, all opposition had to be trampled and destroyed. He neither showed mercy, nor sought it for himself.

It was the only way he had learned to fight in the tough mining camps and sordid saloons of the West. Dempsey never fought for sport, but for survival.

He retained that desperate, cruel streak when massacring Jess Willard, he was sadistic when flooring the huge Firpo nine times, and merciless when crushing Georges Carpentier. Only when Tunney came along was the Old Mauler neither desperate nor hungry and was, therefore, stripped of his greatness.

For colour and personality, Dempsey leaves Tunney and Louis at the post. To-day at 58 the Old Mauler is more popular than when he was champion. The American fight crowd show greater affection for him than Louis or the present champion, Rocky Marciano.

Dempsey's popularity has grown with the years. It is typical of human fickleness that, although the Manassa gladiator was the biggest box-office attraction the ring has ever produced, he was unpopular with crowds when he first won his title. They loved his brutality, and yet were afraid of it.

He had become so invincible as a slayer of his fellow pugilists that the crowd went with the underdog, paying millions of dollars, always hoping but never believing someday an opponent would give the champ the hiding of his life.

Yet when it finally happened and Tunney dethroned him in 1926 after he had reigned supreme for seven years, fight fans all but wept. Nine out of ten Americans wanted Dempsey to regain the title when the pair met again a year later.

Dempsey in defeat had risen to even greater heights than in victory. He had returned to his suite in a Philadelphia hotel two hours after the sporting world had been shocked as the news had been flashed that he had been beaten by Tunney. He was almost unrecognisable. One side of his face was black and blue. One eye was completely hidden beneath puffed and purple flesh. His lips were bruised and bloody.

Reporters, friends, and the usual hangers-on that boxing seems to breed, jammed into the huge suite where a great victory party was to have been held.

Dempsey looked a pitiful sight. His body ached and his brain was numbed by the shock at finding he was no longer invincible. He would dearly have loved to have crept into a bed and be left to sleep the clock round. But he carried off defeat like a real champion. His beautiful wife, Estelle Taylor, the film-star, unable to conceal her disappointment, inquired: "What happened, champ?"

Jack shrugged his huge shoulders, forced a lop-sided smile and through puffed and bruised lips, mumbled: "Honey, I guess I forgot to duck."

There were no alibis, and tough newspapermen suddenly

felt full as they punched out their typewritten columns. The humble and simple phrase "I forgot to duck" reached the homes of millionaires and simple folk throughout the world, and Dempsey found a new warm corner in millions of hearts.

The rise of Dempsey from rags to riches is one of the ring's finest romances. No pugilist in history has sprung from such mixed stock. His mother and father, both Mormons, settled at Manassa, Colorado from West Virginia. His father's folk were from County Kildare, Ireland. His mother was a mixture of Scottish, Irish and Indian blood, for her mother was half Cherokee Indian. Furthermore, Dempsey's grandfather, Abraham Levy, was a Jewish pedlar from East Tennessee.

Because his parents were desperately poor, the tall frail youngster they always called Harry—his correct name is William Harrison Dempsey—had to take a job as a boy. The hard work on a farm, in a copper mine, as a lumberjack and as a saloon bar-bouncer fitted him for his more important job—the winning of the heavyweight crown.

Young Dempsey always had the wanderlust. He had a reputation as a scrapper in the mining camps around Colorado and Utah, but his fighting career really began around 1915 when he knocked out most opposition. He was paid only $2.50 for his first fight but in 1916 realised his ambition and arrived in New York.

His début was not successful. He won three fights without impressing, and soon the few dollars he had earned ran out and he couldn't get any more fights. With his first manager John Reisler, known as John the Barber, deciding there wasn't any future in managing this big young fellow, Dempsey found himself unwanted in the big city.

So, with his brother John, he joined the hoboes, hopped a freight car to Philadelphia. For days they haunted the sidewalks with unshaven faces and hungry bellies. Sometimes they tormented themselves, pressing noses against the steamy windows of a cook-shop from whence drifted the appetising smell of such luxuries as Hamburgers, but three cents, which was all the fighter had in his pocket, wouldn't even buy a hot-dog.

And so the Dempsey boys invested their total capital into buying three apples at a cent a time. They split the third one, never dreaming the next time Dempsey was to appear in Philadelphia it would be with a bank roll exceeding 2,000,000 dollars.

The Dempsey luck changed when he hooked up with Doc Kearns. After he had broken with John the Barber and had walked the streets of Philadelphia unable to get fights, he returned to Salt Lake City, but received his biggest ever setback in being knocked out in one round by Jim Flynn, already past his best.

Then, like many other disillusioned pugilists, he "hit the rods" for California where he went to work in the Union Iron Mines. A local fight manager Fred Winsor was interested in his scrapping ability and looked after him for a couple of fights in San Francisco and Oakland, but then he met up with Kearns who, like the fighter, at this time was broke.

The Doc could see possibilities in Dempsey, took him out of the mines and began a ballyhoo programme that was not only to earn millions of dollars for them both, but was also to make Tex Rickard. Without Kearns, Dempsey might never have reached the top and, without Dempsey, there certainly wouldn't have been a Rickard.

Dempsey began to sweep the country with a series of one-round knockouts in 1918. He revenged his defeat by Jim Flynn, putting his conqueror away in one round; Arthur Pelkey, Fred Fulton, Battling Levinsky, Gunboat Smith were also among his K.O. victims. He dropped only one decision over 4 rounds to Willie Meehan.

Kearns soon built Dempsey into the greatest fighter the West had known, and in the summer of 1919 the 24-year-old ex-miner from Manassa was matched with the gigantic champion, Jess Willard of Toledo . . . in a championship battle that was to

46

turn into a blood-battle, and which has gone down in fistic history as the Massacre of Toledo.

Willard, standing 6ft. 6¼ inches, dwarfed his challenger by five inches, and, at 17½ stone, had a weight advantage of more than 4 stone, but the beautifully built young man from Manassa wasn't worried. He went in with the speed of a featherweight and the power of a bulldozer. 20,000 fight fans, who had paid over £100,000, gasped. Never had they seen such a human tornado. Never had a challenger treated a champion with less respect. After two murderous minutes, Willard's face was mashed to pulp. Blood dripped from cuts above both eyes and from his nose. His eyes were puffed, and his lips were split. A right to the jaw sent him tottering to the canvas. It was the first time he had ever been floored in his life.

Six more times in the remaining minute Willard was sent crashing. The crowd went wild, and nobody heard the end of the round. Willard was slumped on the canvas. Blood seemed to drip from every part of his face. He was the victim of a cosh gang as his seconds dragged him to his corner.

Referee Ollie Pecord raised Dempsey's hand after counting out the battered giant from Kansas and declared him the new world champion. Jack, delighted at yet another one-round triumph, sprang over the ropes. Only then was it learned the round had ended and that Dempsey was not yet world champion.

What a pity it was for Willard, because although Dempsey never scaled another knockdown, he simply battered and cut the giant for six more bloody minutes. Dempsey's inexperience showed up in the second round for he had become exhausted from his own efforts to annihilate the champion.

The third session was legalised murder. Dempsey smashed the big cowboy from corner to corner. Willard's right eye was completely closed. The rest of his face was like raw steak . . . a pathetic-looking Frankenstein who stumbled round the ring, who leaned drunkenly on the ropes, holding out two gigantic arms in a feeble attempt to protect his bruised and bleeding face from the fists of his executioner. When the third round ended he was dragged to his corner once more, oblivious of his fate.

Willard did not come up for the fourth. He could not be blamed. He had suffered more pain and anguish in those three rounds than many a fighter has in 20 rounds.

Controversy flared up whether the fight ended in the third or fourth round, but it clearly ended in the third because the bell had not sounded for the fourth. Definite confirmation later came from the time-keeper, W. Warren Barbour. He declared 13 seconds of the minute's rest had still remained.

The Willard massacre swept America and Europe. Dempsey had become the man of the hour. His name was now international.

In 1920 he twice defended his title, knocking out Billy Miske in 3 rounds and Bill Brennan in 12. And then in 1921, Rickard and Kearns ballyhooed the first million-dollar gate between Dempsey and Carpentier, the Frenchman who had won the world light-heavyweight crown a year earlier knocking out Battling Levinsky at Jersey City and had caused devastation among the heavyweights of Europe and England in particular.

Carpentier was a hero, having served in the war with distinction, whereas Dempsey was never more unpopular than at this period. Most of the 80,000 crowd yelled their delight as the handsome and lighter Carpentier was introduced as "A soldier of France." Dempsey was booed and hissed by a large section of the crowd.

The champion grinned wickedly, the hate and resentment of those who jeered him was unleashed on Carpentier, who was outclassed and battered by murderous body blows in four rounds. True, Carpentier landed one great right-handed punch on the Mauler's chin which staggered Dempsey but only momentarily, and Carpentier paid for such impudence.

The most sensational of all Dempsey's battles was against Luis Firpo, the Wild Bull of the Pampas, at the New York Polo Grounds in 1923. 85,000 watched 3 minutes and 57 seconds of the fiercest fighting ever seen. Dempsey himself was knocked clean out of the ropes in the opening round, but was pushed back by friendly boxing writers. The Wild Bull was floored seven times in the first round and twice in the second before being knocked out.

Firpo, a huge hairy creature from Argentina, had little fighting brain, but possessed a terrific wallop. Although given little chance against Dempsey, he came closer than any fighter, apart from Tunney, to dethroning the champion. Twice in the opening minutes he halted the panther-like attacks of Dempsey, stunning the champion with a right hook to the head and a right swing to the body that caused the Manassa Mauler to sag at the knees. Dempsey only prevented himself from going down by grabbing the South American with both gloves.

Then Dempsey took over, and, moving in with a vicious left hook, dropped Firpo. The South American rose immediately and went after the champion. Dempsey loved this sort of fight, and an uppercut dropped the Wild Bull again. Firpo was up and down again five more times, and then came the greatest sensation in any heavyweight title fight.

The Wild Bull was now a Mad Bull. His eyes blazing as he rushed at Dempsey, and with a right swing to the champ's jaw, lifted him back and clean through the ropes. The newspaper men who assisted Dempsey broke the rules, and the champion should have been disqualified but the excitement was such that the referee took no action. Dempsey recovered to survive the round, and Firpo was flattened in the next session. Dempsey was not extended again until Tunney beat him in 1926 at Philadelphia and in the return bout at Chicago in 1927. The consolation to Dempsey was that, in the second fight, he succeeded not only in flooring Tunney for the now historic 14 seconds' count in the seventh round, but in winning more friends than any heavyweight champion before or since.

Dempsey earned well over £1,000,000. Like most champions he had his share of financial and wife troubles, but he not only

49

remained unspoiled but has become more lovable as he has mellowed with the years.

Gene Tunney was the complete contrast of Dempsey. All they had in common was early poverty. His mother and father had left Kiltimagh in County Mayo, Ireland, and emigrated to America because they could barely raise the rent for their little cottage. They settled in New York's Greenwich Village and Gene grew up realising their daily bread had to be earned before it could be eaten.

In the first world war he joined the Marines and became light-heavyweight champion of the American Expeditionary Force in France. In 1918 he was only 20, but decided then he would become heavyweight champion of the world.

He kept winning fights, but many were dull and he lacked the colour and box-office appeal of Dempsey. When the Manassa Mauler defended his title against Carpentier in 1921, Tunney fought Soldier Jones on the same bill. Although Gene won in 7 rounds, the fight was so disappointing that thousands left the arena to take refreshment before the Dempsey fight started.

Tunney studied Dempsey against Carpentier, and although he was disappointed with his own showing he repeated his promise to himself: "I know I can lick that guy."

Tunney's success was due to the fact that he was his own severest critic. After the Soldier Jones bout, he decided he was too heavy, so for weeks he worked out in Stillman's Gym. He purchased books by James J. Corbett, Jim Jeffries and Bob Fitzsimmons, studied their styles, and swotted up literature on anatomy, muscular movement, diet, etc.

Nature had bestowed on Dempsey all the gifts that went to make the perfect heavyweight champion. Not so Tunney. He had to achieve his ambition the hard way, spending years studying, sweating in the gym and imposing rigid self-discipline. He neither drank nor smoked nor, like so many of the champs, sought the company of show girls. Tunney's chart was set towards that heavyweight title, and he was prepared to lead a life of monastic self-denial until his goal was reached.

He won the American light-heavyweight title from Battling Levinsky in 1922, lost it to the great Harry Greb the same year, but regained it again twice beating Greb in 1923, and stopping Carpentier in 1924. The decision he dropped to Greb was the only fight he ever lost.

Tunney refused to be hustled into a Dempsey fight—just as he managed his various managers rather than allow them to take charge. He hired Dempsey's sparring partners, read books about the Mauler, studied Dempsey films. All this time, the champion was having a good time, not bothering about training.

When Gene considered the time was ripe to pluck Dempsey, he accepted Tex Rickard's offer. "I had Dempsey in a test tube by now," "Professor" Gene told me, when we chatted about his success some months after he had won the title. "I knew every move he would make, and every weakness he had."

Tunney approached this biggest fight in his career with nerves of ice, and certainly shook Dempsey and nearly gave Rickard ulcers by announcing he was flying in from his training camp to Philadelphia. Air travel in 1926 wasn't considered the safest way to keep a date with a world champion, but it had its desired effect in shaking Dempsey, causing him to ponder "What sort of a guy is this?"

For the return bout in Chicago, Tunney demanded and received £200,000 for 30 minutes' boxing. He had one more fight against Tom Heeney, and then kissed the fight game farewell, marrying an heiress.

To-day Tunney at 55 is a millionaire and president of several wealthy companies. He is not popular like Dempsey, but can sit back among his millions, snug in the knowledge that of all the great Kings of the Ring he alone used the fight game to suit his ends, and that he had the strength of character to refuse a million dollars when tempted to make a come-back.

CHAPTER V

GHOST WITH A HAMMER IN HIS HAND

THE MOST EXTRAORDINARY pugilist ounce for ounce I ever set
my eyes on was Jimmy Wilde. The phenomenal little Welshman
who was not a flyweight and scarcely paperweight was aptly
enough dubbed the Tylorstown Terror and the Mighty Atom.
But Pedlar Palmer, the old "Box of Tricks," coined a nom de
guerre that described Wilde even more accurately—the Ghost
with a Hammer in his hand!

Wilde was indeed a fistic ghost who never in his prime
exceeded 7st. 4lbs. A phantom who when stripped was the
nearest living thing to a skeleton, yet when he went into action
became a ring slayer.

I shall never cease to be astonished all these years after when
my memory turns back to the hundreds of fights I saw Wilde
take part in, scaling between 6st. 10lbs. and 7st. 4lbs. His
starchy complexion, drum-stick arms and pipe-stem legs caused
National Sporting Club members to retire to the bar when
Wilde made his first appearance in the Club in a trial bout
with tough Joe Wilson of Stepney. Yet he massacred the
world's best flyweights (8 stone), bowled over good bantams
(8st. 6lbs.) and, not infrequently, flattened a leading featherweight (9 stone). Wilde didn't pick out the "mugs" from the
heavier divisions as his victims either. Only the best was good
enough for the Mighty Atom.

What makes Wilde even more remarkable is that he tore up
every textbook and defied the orthodox style laid down by Jem
Mace. He was personally helped by Jim Driscoll who polished
up some of the rougher edges, but Jimmy refused to ape
Peerless Jim, and frequently shattered the first principle of the

52

Art of Self-Defence by leading with his right. I can see him now in the National Sporting Club looking under-nourished and sickly, crouching in the ring with both gloves resting on his thighs. The portrait of a stable-lad who had never had a glove on in his life before if you like, but a fighter—never! Yes, that was Jimmy Wilde who, despite his freakish physical appearance was a born champion and a natural hitter, because Nature had bestowed on him the gift every athlete covets—the art of perfect timing. Wilde at 7 stone punched harder than most featherweights. With patience a novice can learn to box, but no man can be taught how to punch. Either he can, or he can't.

Perhaps the finest tribute to Wilde is that although he lost but 4 of 864 bouts, he was never more loved or respected than in the two most bloodiest battles of his career when he himself was knocked out in London by Pete Herman of America, the greatest bantam I ever saw, and by Pancho Villa, the little Filipino, in New York. After receiving concussion when his head crashed on the edge of the ring in the Herman fight, Wilde took several counts but refused to stay down until finally that great referee, Jack Smith, picked him up gently as though handling a Dresden China piece, tucked the little game-cock under his arm and deposited him with equal tenderness on his stool. "I had to pick you up Jimmy," said Smith thickly, as he fought back a tear "because you just don't know the way to stay down."

Two years passed before Wilde fought again. This time he came out of unofficial retirement to tackle Villa. He was now through, not having recovered from the Herman beating. The Filipino battered him in seven rounds, and again he was concussed, but although Jimmy knew he didn't stand a chance against Villa, his last instruction before leaving his corner to his chief second Benny Williams was: "No matter what happens to me, Benny, you must not throw in the towel. If I'm going to lose my title I want to go fighting—until I can't stand up any more."

How many champions lost their titles fighting to the last

breath in their body? Precious few. Whether Wilde showed wisdom is debatable but he displayed a courage that has seldom been seen since.

These were the only occasions in which Wilde was knocked out, but so great was Jimmy in defeat that he made hundreds of thousands of new friends in Britain and America as the curtain fell on his great career. It isn't difficult to be great in triumph, but Wilde was magnificent in defeat, and remained a champ in the hearts of all fight fans who saw him in the twilight against Herman and Villa. Instead of fading into oblivion after retirement, Wilde's reputation blossomed as the years rolled by.

The fight against Herman took place at the Albert Hall on January 13, 1921. And never did a boxer enter the ring with the odds so heavily loaded against him as did the little Welshman. Wilde, who had enjoyed a successful tour of America and Canada in 1920, had been out of the ring some eight months and was approaching 30. He was not over anxious for this match, but was tempted by the large purse for those days of £8,000 plus £250 training expenses. His manager Teddy Lewis of Pontypridd insisted the money should be deposited in a London bank seven days before the fight.

While Herman and his pilot Sam Goldstein did not take on this precaution and paid dearly for the oversight, the Americans seemed to get the better end of the fight conditions. They insisted on 20 rounds whereas Wilde had requested 15 and, cutely enough, Goldstein demanded a clause in the contract whereby Herman could weigh-in at 2 o'clock and not at the ringside as was the American custom at this time.

The match was made at 8st. 6lbs. Wilde scaled only 7st. 11lbs; Herman weighed-in at 2 o'clock and made the weight. Teddy Lewis protested that the American should climb on the scales again at the ringside immediately before the fight, and slapping his fist on the massage table in Wilde's dressing room, shouted: "Either Herman weighs-in or the fight's off."

But shrewd little Sam Goldstein was equally obstinate. "If that's how you feel, Ted, it's O.K. by us. Pete weighed in as

54

agreed in our contract and he doesn't get back on those scales for you or anybody else. No sir! That's final."

There was a dreadful hullabaloo going on in Wilde's dressing room. The door opened and slammed as an excited official or reporter entered. The hooting from a heated crowd drifted down the corridors. The cheapest seats that night were £3 10s. and the crowd was already angry because Battling Levinsky had been unable to fight Bombardier Billy Wells in a preliminary due to an injured hand. Now the rumour was spreading that Herman would not weigh-in and that the fight might be off.

The young Prince of Wales (now the Duke of Windsor, of course) who had not patronised big boxing before had left his seat at the ringside and climbed into the ring with a tactful few humorous words just at a time when the crowd was getting hostile and unpleasant.

This news came to Jimmy Wilde as he sat on the rubbing table, palefaced and strained, obviously disturbed by the bickering and the noise in his dressing room. He had hardly spoken a word, but now he became angry. "Will you all stop doing the fighting," he shouted, "and get out of here. I don't care what Herman weighs—I'll fight him because I'm not going to let down the Prince of Wales."

The little man, his face now flushed with anger and some emotion, turned to see Lord Lonsdale at the door of his dressing room. The sporting Earl had brought a personal message from the Prince saying he hoped Wilde would go on with the fight.

As Jimmy reached the ringside the Prince leaned forward, shook the boxer by the hand and said: "Thank you, Wilde. Good luck."

The Welshman smiled and replied: "I'll do my best, Your Highness. He'll have to knock me out to win."

Wilde then requested the M.C. to announce that as the match was no longer at 8st. 6lbs. all bets made prior to the fight should be called off. That in itself was significant.

He bowed to the Prince and then slipped through the ropes— a diminutive David of the ring ready to tackle yet another

Goliath, for the dark-haired Herman had refused to weigh-in knowing he was getting on for two stone heavier. And this against the world's best bantam. A fighter who was heavier and younger and whose skill, cunning and tigerish ferocity matched Wilde. He was a super-scrapper and no man living could have given him half a stone—far less than nearly two stone.

The little Welshman probably realised this in the first round, and certainly in the second round when Herman almost knocked him out with a vicious uppercut. But because Wilde was a great champion he recovered so magnificently that at the end of fifteen rounds he had done enough to earn the decision. If only the Herman camp had not insisted on 20 rounds!

But Herman was stronger and paced himself like a great King of the Ring. He knew Wilde's strength was running out as fast as sugar from a split sack, and in the 17th round Herman caught the tired Welshman with one of Wilde's own specialities—he led with his right and sent Jimmy reeling across the ring to crash through the middle ropes, the back of his head hitting the canvas with a sickening thud. A blow that was subsequently to rob him of his world title and to end his wonderful career. Yet he climbed up only to be knocked down again until the referee stopped the slaughter.

Against Pancho Villa, Wilde was just a Ghost . . . and the hammer in his hand had gone. With two years of idleness and nearly 32, his reflexes, ring judgement and his footwork were just memories. Jimmy knew this but the £13,000 offer to defend his world title at Polo Grounds, New York was too much of a temptation, and so he took another battering and won the admiration of the 40,000 crowd. After being knocked down after the bell at the end of the second round with a rabbit punch, Jimmy fought on his mind a complete blank and was knocked out in the seventh.

So mashed was the little man who didn't know the meaning of the word surrender, unable to see out of either eye, that when the brown-skinned Villa came into the dressing room he burst into tears and, turning to Wilde's wife, sobbed in broken

English: "So sorry. Me no wanted to hurt him." Wilde was critically ill and took months to recover. He never fought again, but in spite of his suffering he was more fortunate than either of his victors.

Poor Pancho Villa died two years afterwards, while still world champion, after having a tooth damaged in a fight with Jimmy McLarnin. And Pete Herman—although retaining active interest in boxing as a member of the Louisiana State Athletic Commission—is blind. To this day he says his toughest battle was not against a bantamweight, but against a little Welsh guy named Jimmy Wilde.

But don't let the greatness of Wilde in defeat take from his brilliance in victory, for he was a pugilistic phenomenon, a genius of the ring.

I first heard of him in 1910 from the self-styled Professor Joe Smith, a boxing promoter in London's East End, and one of the first to promote at the old Wonderland. "I was in Wales last week," said the Professor, "and in Jack Scarrott's booth I saw the most amazing kid in my life. His name is Wilde. He's just 5 stone, but he's knocking out flyweights, bantams and feathers."

I didn't pay undue heed for although Joe Smith was a splendid judge of talent, I believed at this time that he was over-enthusiastic. I always said that hungry fighters make the only worthwhile champions. Well, Jimmy was hungry enough. Before he was thirteen he had left school to go into the Ferndale coal pits to earn two shillings a day.

He married in his teens, and when his wife Lisbeth and himself were broke they tramped the Rhondda Valley selling red hearth stones to provide themselves with the bare necessities. Wilde maintains without his wife he would never have become a champion. In his early days she even acted as his sparring partner, wearing a shield over her chest.

One day when working at the pit-head he slipped and was caught beneath a fast-moving cable which gashed his right leg so severely that for a week after there were fears of an amputation. To this day the Mighty Atom carries a cavity above his ankle.

Wilde was a born fighter, but he was most certainly developed in Jack Scarrott's travelling booth when he had several hundred fights. One morning he knocked out seventeen opponents, and at two o'clock Scarrott, who died only six years ago in his 85th year, came over and said: "You must be tired, my boy, go and have a bite of lunch." The lunch consisted of a bun and a cup of tea. Within ten minutes Scarrott was calling for Jimmy again, and the boy knocked out eight more victims. For knocking out 23 opponents that day, Scarrott gave Jimmy 15/- and Wilde was happy. It was as much as he earned in the mines in a week.

A year after Professor Joe Smith's enthusiastic forecast, Wilde, who was born at Quaker's Yard, Tylorstown, had his first fight in London and knocked out Matt Wells' Nipper in one round.

He returned to Wales and won fight after fight, and continued to bowl over flyweights and bantamweights in 1913 and 1914 until he won the British flyweight title in November 1914, out-pointing the hard-hitting champion, Joe Symonds of Plymouth.

Wilde surprisingly lost his title a couple of months later to Tancy Lee when he retired in 17 rounds. It was the Welshman's gameness and obstinacy that made him go through with the fight and stay on his feet for 17 rounds. He was not fit, and how he passed the doctor is beyond me. He was in bed a couple of days before the fight but refused to postpone it.

Lee punched his weight that night. After the bout, Wilde was taken to a hotel near the N.S.C. with his left ear mashed to pulp. One of his party wanted to cut off a hanging piece with a penknife but fortunately Ralph Lyle, a well-known Cardiff sportsman, had intervened.

Lee lost his title to Joe Symonds and in 1916 Wilde regained the crown beating Symonds again—this time in 11 rounds. A few months later he revenged the defeat by Tancy Lee stopping the Scot also in 11 rounds.

In December 1916, the Welshman became the first official world flyweight champion when he stopped Young Zulu Kid, an Italian-American, in 11 rounds at the Holborn Stadium. He joined the Army Gymnastic Staff as a sergeant-instructor, and when he put up one of the greatest performances of his career by stopping Joe Conn, a top-grade Hebrew featherweight, at Stamford Bridge in 1918 he did so for a small bag of diamonds because a Colonel had refused him permission to box for money!

Wilde was at his greatest in 1919 when he beat the American Joe Lynch at the National Sporting Club and Pal Moore at Olympia. Lynch later beat Pete Herman to win the world bantam crown, although Pete regained it later. Moore, incidentally, was the only fighter, besides Tancy Lee, Herman and Villa, to beat Wilde. He had gained a three-round decision in the bantam final of the Inter-Allied tournament at the Albert Hall in 1918. It was a bad verdict and the crowd were so angry that it took R.S.M. Jim Driscoll to climb into the ring to appease them. Driscoll said simply: "Listen, lads, the judges have said Moore is the winner. You must stand by that decision."

Wilde was not satisfied until he got Moore back in the ring, and in 1919 at Olympia outpointed him over 20 rounds.

When Jimmy finally hung up his gloves after the Villa fight, it was the passing of a great school of Welsh fighters—men like Tom Thomas, Jim Driscoll and Freddie Welsh.

Wilde, Driscoll and Welsh were the greatest fighters Wales ever produced and Wilde the most remarkable of this trio. Freddy Welsh—his correct name was Frederick Hall Thomas —was an enigma. He was never the good mixer that Driscoll was, but what a great battler.

Welsh really learned to fight in America and his first serious bouts took place at Philadelphia in 1905 when he was 18. The Americans went wild over him. And so did Britain when he returned in 1907 to beat the best opposition in the country.

Freddy remained undefeated until 1908 when he dropped a decision to the great Packy McFarland. He fought a 20-round draw with McFarland at Los Angeles a few months later and again at the National Sporting Club in 1909. I must say that in this third fight McFarland was a good winner. For the first time in the history of the N.S.C. there were threats shouted at the referee, Mr. Tom Scott. Even members in evening dress brandished walking sticks and acted more like a mob. A rumour spread that Scott had been "got at" by bookmakers because a well-known Dublin public man had backed McFarland to win for several thousand pounds. Anyway, whatever the reason, Scott only refereed a novices' competition some weeks later, and not long afterwards was taken to a mental institution where he died.

Welsh had two great scraps with Matt Wells, who had won the A.B.A. title four times. Wells took the title off Freddy in 1911, but Welsh had his revenge when he outpointed Matt over 20 rounds a year later. There was much dispute about this verdict.

In 1914 Welsh brought the world's lightweight crown to Britain when he clearly outpointed the American champion, Willie Ritchie, at Olympia, London. Freddy agreed to fight for practically nothing to get the world title—and he got nothing out of the fight at all. Ritchie's camp had demanded of Charles B. Cochran a guarantee of 28,000 dollars and Freddy agreed to take what remained. There was nothing left.

Freddy lost his title to Benny Leonard in New York, 1917, when a little sharp practice was adopted. It was a "No-Decision" bout, and although Leonard was having the better of the fight, Welsh could not have lost his title unless he was knocked out. The referee stopped the bout in the ninth with only one round to go. The title was snatched from him.

Poor Welsh was unlucky most of his life. His physical culture school and training camp at Summit, New Jersey failed, and so every penny he had earned the hard way with his fists and blood went up in smoke. In 1927 he died broke in a New York apartment. He died quite alone.

CHAPTER VI

JINX FIGHTER OF BRITISH CHAMPIONS

NO FOREIGN INVADER has ever caused such complete devastation and demoralisation of British boxing than handsome, debonair Georges Carpentier. No other pugilist from France, the rest of Europe or even the United States has ever held so many of our champions to the ridicule of their own countrymen as did this Beau Brummel from the Champs-Élysées.

In fact, if there hadn't been an England with its colourful Bombardier Billy Wells and its sullen but hard-punching Joe Beckett, Georges Carpentier would never have won an immortal place in Boxing's Hall of Fame. Gorgeous Georges was certainly the Gravedigger of British Champions. He licked them all—most of them in quick time—Young Joseph (10 rounds); Billy Wells (twice—in 4 and 1); Beckett (twice—in 1); Jim Sullivan (2); George Cook (4); Ted Kid Lewis (1); Dick Smith (8); Pat O'Keefe (2). But it was a different story against tough American babies like the Dixie Kid, Frank Klaus, Billy Papke, Gene Tunney, Tommy Loughran and, of course, Dempsey who thrashed the Frenchman in four rounds in the first-ever million-dollar heavyweight championship in 1921.

Carpentier was a born fighter. He began boxing as an amateur at 12, was tackling men at thirteen, and taking part in 20 round bouts at 14. His great secret was that he possessed the fastest right-hand punch I have seen in more than fifty years of watching the greatest of them all come and go. As lightning flashes—or as the cobra strikes—so did the handsome Frenchman's right hand connect, usually before his victims had even sensed danger. In his two bouts with Beckett, Carpentier punched almost faster than sound . . . sound of the gong at any rate.

Equally important towards his success was his complete ruthlessness inside the ring. He was the smiling matinee idol on the streets of London. The heart-throb of every woman boxing fan—and Carpentier more than any other pugilist attracted women to his big fights thirty and forty years ago—as he ducked under the ropes in a magnificent gown, not a single hair out of place, and the flashing smile of a good-humoured schoolboy as, most meticulously, he bowed to his male admirers and blew kisses to his female worshippers.

But beneath that mask of charm was the mean streak of the Apache. Once the gong had sounded Carpentier was a killer—ruthless and unscrupulous. To Carpentier the roped arena was a jungle and he believed the only way to survive was to toss every ounce of strength in his body, pull out every trick he knew until all opposition had been trampled under and his foe was lying prostrate at his feet.

Perhaps this is to Carpentier's credit because the fight game is cruel and the ring no hot-house for orchids. A great champion should not know the meaning of mercy and must be mean. That was the difference between the successful French-man and lovable Billy Wells. Yet admitting all this, the Frenchman's ruthlessness trespassed dangerously at times on the borders of bad sportsmanship as in his controversial fights with Ted Kid Lewis, George Cook and the tough American Gunboat Smith.

The partnership of Descamps and Carpentier was the greatest fistic combination the ring has known . . . far more successful than the Dempsey-Kearns set-up. It was the little French character who made Carpentier into a great fighter. And it was Descamps who used every trick—fair and foul—to save his Georges when things were not going right.

Carpentier, like our own Len Harvey, fought at every weight —from 8 stone up to the heavy division. I first met him before the first world war when Descamps brought him as a skinny youngster to London. He was invited to spar with Billy Wells and in spite of the French youngster's determination and enthusiasm few of us dreamed in a few years he would be good enough to whip Wells twice.

I have often read that Carpentier worked down a coal-mine at Lens. This is not true. His father was a miner and Georges was brought up in a tough environment which may explain some of his less pleasant tactics inside the ring. His first job was a cycle messenger for which he was paid a few francs a week.

He was later employed in the offices of the coal company at Lens when Descamps, a clown in a travelling circus, discovered him. In 1911 when only 17 his reputation had reached London when he won the French welterweight championship and soon afterwards had his first fights in England beating Sid Burns over 15 rounds and knocked out Young Joseph in 10 to win the European welterweight crown.

Two years later when only 19 he met Billy Wells at Ghent. Weighing at least three stone lighter and several inches shorter, he shocked our fight fans by knocking out the British heavy-weight champion in 4 rounds.

This fight was a perfect example of what a mysterious fighter Wells was; he should have won because, as then, I still insist the handsome Bombardier had more ability than Carpentier and a better punch. In the first minute he sent the French lad crashing to the canvas. The timekeeper either favoured Carpentier or became over-excited, because the late J. T. Hulls insisted afterwards Georges was down for 14 seconds. When Carpentier struggled up every ounce of blood had drained from his face, his eyes were frightened and he staggered stupidly like a drunken man. A third-rate heavyweight or an alert light-weight could have bowled over this lurching but easy target. But not Wells, the enigma. Instead of going in, Billy stood back as though sorry for what he had done to a smaller and younger man.

Carpentier, always game, recovered in the second round and, now minus his mask of charm, was snarling as he dug sharp rights into the Bombardier's body—always his weak section. The Frenchman was well on top by the fourth round. There certainly wasn't any reciprocation for the mercy Wells had foolishly shown him in that first round. Carpentier seizing every chance, sank a murderous right to Wells' body and then flashed over that jet-like right again to the Bombardier's long pointed chin, and the heavyweight champion of Britain was flattened by a French lad who weighed little more than a middleweight.

Although this result embarrassed sportsmen back home, 29 nights later Wells successfully defended his British title beating Packy Mahony of Cork in 13 rounds. Wells then defeated Pat O'Keefe at the Blackfriars Ring and Gunner Jim Moir in 5 rounds at the Canterbury Music Hall in Westminster Bridge Road. This latest win put the Bombardier back in the market and there was clamour to bring Carpentier to London to prove that what had happened to our champion in Belgium was but a fluke. The match was made at the National Sporting Club on December 8, 1913—six months after the first meeting.

I can picture this return bout as though it happened only yesterday. The distinguished crowd were in good humour and confident of a Wells victory. I remember staring at the silk hat of the timekeeper Mr. E. Zerega who sat on a dais outside the ring. He pushed the switch of the electric bell, and every one of us inside the club was tense and excited. Carpentier came out of his corner like a greyhound out of a trap. In complete contrast to last time, the lighter Frenchman did not have a hair of his well-groomed head displaced. He sank left and right digs to Wells' body and, to the discomfort of everyone present, the Bombardier suddenly folded like a puppet and took the full count after only 18 seconds. Carpentier had reduced our heavyweight champion to a laughing stock and the Corinthians, although red-faced with embarrassment, like true British sportsmen, applauded the conquering hero from across the English Channel.

Yet the remarkable Bombardier Billy, who had the ability

The end of Jack Johnson's reign. The long search for a "White Hope" ends when Jess Willard, a gigantic cowboy from Kansas, knocks out Johnson in 26 rounds at Havana, Cuba, on April 5, 1915. Some cynics insist that Johnson is shading the sun from his eyes while the referee counts him out.

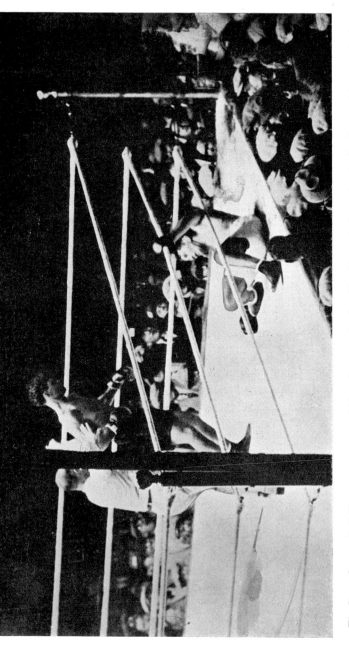

The Long Count. Jack Dempsey comes to within a few seconds of making history by becoming the first heavyweight to regain the world title. Tunney is down in the 7th round but the referee refuses to count until Dempsey retreats to a neutral corner. It is estimated that Tunney was on the canvas for 14 seconds due to Dempsey's impetuosity. Gene went on to retain the title on points.

but not the temperament or wickedness to become a world champion, did not lose his popularity after this. He continued to win fights beating Gunner Rawles, Bandsman Rice (twice) and Bandsman Blake until he was knocked out in 10 rounds by Frank Moran, the Pittsburgh dentist renowned for his "Mary Ann" right-hand wallop. Even this defeat didn't stop Wells from topping the bill and he was as popular as ever when beating Dick Smith (three times), Dick Rice, Petty-Officer Curran and Dan Voyles. By beating Voyles at the N.S.C., the Bombardier won outright the first Lonsdale belt for the heavyweight division.

Carpentier had only one more fight in London after the k.o. of Wells before war broke out. This was against Gunboat Smith at Olympia in July, 1914, and he was lucky to keep up his record of never losing a fight in Britain. The French fighter was caught off-balance after swinging a dangerous right which missed by inches. He slipped to the ground as Gunboat—so called because he wore size 13 boots—was attacking and was unable to stop himself, landing another light blow. Descamps acted immediately. He screamed at his fighter to stay down, and then scrambled through the ropes and did a war-dance of his own protesting his "poor Georges" had been brutally fouled. He impressed the English referee Eugene Corri sufficiently because the Gunboat was disqualified . . . a harsh decision I thought. Another uproar followed because Jim Buckley, Smith's pilot, demanded Carpentier be disqualified as Descamps had broken the rules by entering the ring before any decision had been made.

Buckley was still trying to get a re-match when the German armies marched into Belgium. With the war on, Carpentier joined the French Air Force and served with distinction as a pilot.

1919 was a boom year for boxing in Britain. The late C. B. Cochran bought the lease of the Holborn Stadium from Clarence Hatry and opened up in February, 1919, by matching Billy Wells, still heavyweight champion and as popular as ever, with Joe Beckett. Wells still believed he could beat Carpentier, but Cochran insisted he must first defend his title against Arthur Townley, Frank Goddard, Jack Curphey or Beckett. Jim Maloney, who was managing Wells at this time, chose Beckett and asked for £1,000, but Cochran beat Maloney down to £300 and paid Beckett the same.

Cochran invited Carpentier to the ringside, and Georges did nothing but shout advice to "Billee Wells." But Beckett, for my money, was a good heavyweight. His left hook was the best I have seen and, apart from two disastrous fights against Carpentier, his record is good. He punched too hard for the Bombardier that night. Three times in the fifth round Wells was smashed to the canvas by that left hook. Wells remained down the third time.

Although the National Sporting Club refused to recognise Beckett as champion because the bout had not taken place at the club, he was accepted as title holder by sportsmen everywhere, and after beating Frank Goddard in 2 rounds and Eddie McGoorty in 17, both at Olympia, Beckett's stock was extremely high and Cochran signed him to meet Carpentier at Holborn Stadium on December 4 of the same year. The Frenchman's share was £5,000 and Beckett was to receive £3,000.

There was an outcry when the unpretentious little hall, which held only 2,000, was chosen for a fight that would have drawn 50,000, but Olympia was not available. So Cochran took a gamble and charged the unheard of prices of twenty-five guineas ringside and five guineas standing room. These prices stand as a record to this day, and the £30,000 that Cochran drew at Holborn remained a record until Jack Solomons came in on the boxing boom at the end of the second world war.

I went to Charing Cross Station to meet Carpentier on his arrival, but couldn't get near him without assistance from the police. The forecourt was choked with men, women and children, and the Strand was jammed with sightseers, just like a royal procession, as Georges, seated in a landau drawn by bay horses with coachman and valet on the box-seat, acknowledged the cheers of an estimated 30,000 who had turned out to cheer him as he passed by.

What a difference from the end of the second war. Carpentier watched a tournament at Manchester, and was not given a single cheer even though the charges that he had collaborated with the Germans had been disproved.

Outside the Holborn Stadium thousands of fans, either unable to pay the luxury prices or unable to get hold of a ticket, queued for a glimpse of the two fighters arriving. Cordons of police were set up and only those with tickets were allowed to approach anywhere near the stadium.

The Prince of Wales, George Bernard Shaw and Arnold Bennett were just a few of the personalities I recall taking their seats. Two days before the fight the Frenchman had been bitten by a mosquito and when it became badly swollen both Descamps and his trainer, Gus Wilson, pleaded for a postponement, but Carpentier would not listen. The rumour soon spread and Beckett was fancied by the majority of fight fans.

Mr. Bernard John Angle, who 31 years earlier had refereed the bout between John L. Sullivan and Charley Mitchell at Chantilly, called the men to the ropes and explained the rules in English and French. How ironical this proved to be. The bell clanged. Beckett, who looked in wonderful shape, went in aggressively enough in an attempt to plant that left hook that had stopped so many of his own countrymen, but the Frenchman, the smile he had given the Prince, now completely wiped from his face, looked about as friendly as a wounded tiger. He sprang backwards. Beckett went after him to land a body punch, but clinched. "Break!" demanded Jack Angle. They stepped back and then Beckett tried an uppercut and missed. No man could afford to miss against the man with the fastest right hand in the business. He smashed that fist to Beckett's unprotected chin. The fight of the year was all over in 73 seconds. Beckett and 2,000 boxing fans were stunned. Throats were paralysed because only silence greeted the farcical humilation of yet another of our champions by this Bogeyman from France.

In October, 1920, Carpentier made his first trip to America and won the world light-heavyweight title knocking out Battling Levinsky in 4 rounds. He took America by storm and was quickly named Gorgeous Georges and the French Orchid. He was a war hero, too, having been decorated for his deeds in the air, and so the ballyhoo began for his world heavyweight championship fight with Dempsey on July 2, 1921. Tex Rickard built a special structure on a Jersey City swamp known as Boyle's Thirty Acres. The fight drew 80,000 spectators who paid close on £500,000—the first million-dollar gate in the history of boxing.

Dempsey was unpopular at this time because of his failure to join the U.S. Forces during the war. The M.C. introduced them thus: "Georges Carpentier, a soldier of France" . . . and then "Jack Dempsey."

The Frenchman was cheered, Dempsey booed. Sentiment can't win fights however, and apart from a split second mid-way through round 2 when the light Frenchman cracked the same kind of right he had landed on Beckett's chin and Dempsey staggered momentarily, it wasn't a match and the Manassa Mauler battered him about the body and outclassed him in four rounds. Once again a good big 'un had licked a good little 'un. At least the Frenchman received £50,000 share of the purse as a consolation!

Carpentier was back in London at the beginning of 1922 to knock out George Cook, the young Australian, who had impressed when beating Jack Curphey and Frank Goddard. Cook put up a good show and worried Carpentier for three rounds, but in the fifth the Frenchman's right connected on the Australian's chin, but as he had almost crashed forward Carpentier's astonishing right hand had sneaked another blow on the chin settling the fight beyond all doubt. There was booing and protests that Carpentier should have been disqualified. That is history, but how many other fighters could strike two killing rights in a matter of split seconds?

The Frenchman was involved in a similar heated argument when a few months later he was awarded a one-round knockout win over Ted Kid Lewis. Carpentier the Ruthless, taking advantage of the boxing rule that a contestant must defend himself at all times, cracked his dreaded right on Lewis's chin while The Kid was still glancing at the referee after he had spoken to both boxers. The crowd hooted Carpentier for his tactics, but he was awarded the fight.

The biggest upset in Carpentier's career was when he lost his world light-heavyweight crown to the untamed Senegalese former dish-washer Battling Siki in Paris four months after the Kid Lewis bout. I travelled to Paris for this Sunday afternoon bout, convinced I was making a wasted journey because the kinky pompadoured Negro had never before met an opponent of Carpentier's class.

Paris acclaimed its idol as he made his usual debonair entrance, and everybody was in a happy mood prepared to watch the Gorgeous One chop up the Negro. There was, in fact, a persistent rumour that Descamps had done a private cash deal with Siki for Carpentier to win inside six rounds and that Georges had done little training.

What a shock hit the whisperers for, although Georges knocked the Senegalese off his feet in the opening round for 6 and was again floored in the next session for 9, Siki rose to his feet, his black ugly face having assumed the snarl of a beast of the jungle.

He tore into Carpentier with demoniac fury, swinging both fists, inflicting murderous punishment that brought blood from the many cuts on George's handsome face. It was obvious to the experienced student of boxing that Carpentier had neglected his training. He failed to stem the mad rushes the Negro kept up with unceasing ferocity and by the sixth round had his opponent half-blinded and battered. It was an unbelievable climax.

69

Georges could barely stand upright. He reeled backwards unable to defend himself and Siki, his face contorted like a devil's, tossed another of his bone-shattering left hooks and sent Carpentier crashing to the ropes. He slumped to the canvas and was lying there almost unconscious when the referee, Henri Bernstein, announced he had disqualified the Senegalese for throwing Carpentier. Immediately the fashionable crowd raised their voices in protest. Bernstein had made an awful mistake. The rules of the French Boxing Association render it imperative for a referee to consult with the judges before making any such decision and after a quick consultation M. Victor Breyer, a fine sportsman and President of the Federation, climbed into the ring and announced that the decision had been reversed—Siki was world champion.

Carpentier, a sorry mess, had been carried from the ring believing he had won. It was hours before he was told the truth. He was broken hearted when he said to me afterwards: "This Siki is terrible. He is a monster."

Carpentier and Descamps both declared to me in emphatic language that they were not double-crossed. Georges, shrugging his shoulders, said he himself was to blame for not taking his training seriously.

A few years ago I was motored to the death-sounding Hell's Kitchen in New York to be shown the spot where Siki was found murdered after a gang brawl a few days before Christmas, 1925. Nobody knew who had done the deed. Nobody cared. Indeed a tragic ending for a man who not only won a world boxing title, but who had fought through the first world war with such distinction that he was awarded the Croix de Guerre for bravery in action.

After his success over Carpentier, Siki became a strutting gorilla on the boulevards of Paris, terrorising the citizens with two lions on a leash and firing a gun in the air. I remember sitting in the American bar of a restaurant along the Champs Élysées with Jack Smith, the Manchester referee. On the wall was a framed photograph of Dempsey. In walked Siki looking for trouble. He took one glance at the picture and shouted: "Heem champion! No, not heem . . . me!" Then he crashed his fist into the glass smashing the frame into a hundred pieces. This was too much for a small American who was chewing a cigar as he sat on a stool at the bar counter. He quietly climbed down from his seat and, lifting the three-legged stool high to the ceiling, crashed it with sickening force on the back of Siki's skull, knocking him completely out. Still with the cheroot between his lips and the blood streaming across the floor from the gash he had inflicted on the negro's head, the little American calmly pushed his way through the swing doors without so much as a glance at the unconscious figure lying on the floor.

Five months later Siki was spirited away by boat to Dublin to defend his world crown against Mike McTigue, the clever boxer from County Clare, at the Scala Theatre on, of all times, St. Patrick's night. McTigue had for many years made a big reputation in America and had returned to his homeland at the height of the rebellion. Machine-guns rattled and bombs exploded. Carpentier and Descamps were there—they wanted to see Michael kill Siki.

Inside the Scala, everyone was in a nervous tension. We were searched for arms on entering. But the fight itself was a tame affair. The Irishman had skill but no punch and after a disappointing show Jack Smith gave the decision to McTigue.

At midnight we were allowed to leave the building and Smith tried to stop a taxi to take us back to our hotel. The driver ignored the signal and went on hell-for-leather. A few seconds later a Mills bomb hurtled into the cab and a terrific explosion followed. Jack Smith and I gripped each other firmly by the hand. We had nearly taken a death ride together.

Although battered and humiliated by Siki, Carpentier returned to London a year later for his second fight with Beckett which was to prove more humiliating than the bout three years earlier.

71

A month before the fight I stayed for a week with Carpentier at La Guerche where Descamps had a magnificent chateau. One afternoon I accompanied them on a shooting expedition. Georges was a deadly shot, but whilst taking a "pot" at a hare —he already had bagged a dozen—the barrel of the gun burst. It was a miracle Georges was not seriously injured. He laughed and turning to me said: "That was a lucky escape, Jimee. If my arm had been smashed then I should not again be able to knock out Beckett."

Georges frequently found it convenient not to understand English. I have seen all sorts of people trying to extract information from him. He would look bewildered and exclaim: "Je ne comprends pas!" He could speak English like a native!

And so to the night of the fight. Beckett had piled up a number of victories, and Carpentier was considered on the way out, but a not too well trained Beckett was once more held to ridicule by the speed of that right hand and the bout was over in 15 seconds. Beckett never fought again.

The Frenchman returned to America in 1924 but was stopped by Gene Tunney. When he lost to Tommy Loughran in 1926 he had reached the end of the trail. He had lost the speed of his right hand, and not even the tricks of Descamps could now serve him.

To-day at 59 he has a bar in Paris just off the Champs Élysées, but whereas his manager Descamps, who died whilst watching his son playing football, left £20,000, the fortune he earned with his fists disappeared many years ago in various speculations.

But Georges Carpentier will always be remembered as the Jinx Fighter of British Champions. He beat them all . . . and with ridiculous ease.

CHAPTER VII

CLOWN WHO BECAME A CHAMP

As I STEPPED out of the smoky, sweaty atmosphere of the
Brighton gymnasium where Joe Baksi was getting into shape
for his battle with Bruce Woodcock, I was momentarily
blinded by the brilliant sunshine outside. A pipey voice
greeted me: "'Ullo Jimmy Butler. How'y're doing me old
cock sparrow." I could see only a blurred outline of a dapper
figure in a bowler hat and a choker round his neck, but before
I raised one hand to my brow to take the glare from my eyes,
I realised this chirpy greeting had come from old Tom Palmer
. . . better known to fight fans of forty and fifty years ago as
Pedlar Palmer. As my eyes became more accustomed to the
sunshine I was amazed how little this old man had changed
from the days of his prime. He still had those thick black
George Robeyish eye-brows, and beneath them dark eyes
which shone with impudent good humour. And he still cocked
his head perkily on one side like a London sparrow.

As I shook his hand the pleasure that came over his face
could not be concealed. In me he recognised one of the old-
time boxing writers who knew and appreciated his phenomenal
skill in the ring which earned him the title of the "Box of
Tricks." But for younger men the Pedlar was just a little old
man hanging around a gymnasium trying to get a glimpse of
the ring personalities.

Palmer was certainly not there to see the massive Joe Baksi,
because the then 70-year-old former Canning Town bantamweight had no time for the moderns and didn't mince words.
"Come to watch Baksi?" he snapped back to my question.
"Me? Why I wouldn't go in my back yard to watch that big

chunk of flesh. They don't know how to fight any more. They don't know how to feint, to ride a punch. And if you asked the blighters to try the old one-two they would think you were talking blinkin' Chinese."

The Pedlar's visit to the gym was two-fold. He was there to look out for some old-timer of his own generation and to spend a few happy minutes in reminiscence. His other purpose was to borrow the price of a drink. And, as always with him, he took me on one side and whispered into my ear.

I was moved by the Pedlar's plight, because I had known him in the days when he was in the money, and all the wrong boys were bleeding him of every penny he earned. As Palmer became older he would tell glowing stories of the fortune he had won with his fists and had lost or given away. The amount grew as the years went on, and I believe the Pedlar honestly believed he had earned £100,000 and given it away, because that was the figure he frequently quoted to young reporters who occasionally interviewed him.

Had Palmer lived to-day he would certainly have earned that sum and more, but £1,500 was a big championship purse when the Pedlar was holding boxing crowds spellbound with his defensive wizardry.

Palmer was not the finest bantamweight I ever watched, because he was not a big puncher, but he was the greatest character the ring produced, and if you leave aside Jack Johnson and Jim Driscoll, there were few finer defensive boxers. His defence was more spectacular than Driscoll's as he would exaggerate his moves with his bobbing and weaving. And crowds would flock to see him, and laugh aloud as he would pull yet another move from his "box of tricks" and cause an opponent to swing round wildly and miss by feet. I have never seen his equal since. Every time he fought he gave an exaggerated exhibition of boxing science and members of the National Sporting Club loved it. One or two die-hards criticised him for his exhibitionism saying: "He could make all these moves once, but he goes back and does it all over again

74

just to show off." What they forgot was that Tom Palmer was a born entertainer. Because at the turn of the nineteenth century when variety was the rage of the theatre, a little insignificant act that usually managed to get squeezed somewhere near the bottom of the bill was the "Palmer Brothers— Midget Boxing Act."

Tom, then a boy, was the comedian of the turn. His brother Matt chased him round the ring, and Tom slipped punches, turned somersaults, and produced so many tricks that the crowd would roar their heads off. It wasn't until he began to grow and get stronger that it was realised he was not only an acrobat, but a really good boxer.

When he was only 18 he stepped into the National Sporting Club ring to face Walter Croot, one of England's best bantams. Palmer sat in his corner, oblivious of his experienced opponent, and then glanced casually round the club slowly eyeing the stage and members like a youngster who is seeing the Tower of London for the first time, and doesn't want to miss anything.

The fact that the new boy was not given a chance against Croot did not worry Palmer. Even as the gong sounded he still did not appear to be aware of the reputation of his opponent, for he danced from his corner to the centre of the ring with a whimsical little smile and all the cheek of a canary hopping into the cat's saucer of milk to take a drink.

Within a few seconds, astonished members were glancing at each other as though unable to believe their eyes. Here was a boy more like an acrobat or a clown than a fighter. He never remained still for one split second. It was as though the ring canvas was red-hot beneath his feet. He ducked and dodged, bobbed and weaved, and did everything he had done as a child in his variety act . . . everything except turn somersaults.

And all the time he was feinting, and slipping light lefts and rights at the astonished Croot's head. It was a dazzling display of non-stop ringcraft, the like of which had never previously been seen in the club. They never thought this human jack-in-the-box could keep it up against a fighter so experienced and as

75

classy as Croot. When the kid unwinds, Croot will chop him to pieces, was the general opinion. But the Pedlar never unwound that night. Croot having got over his first astonishment was now waiting, his eyes intent, his jaw set grimly, to catch this will-o-the-wisp with one Sunday Punch. You could almost read his mind. "This can't go on for ever." Suddenly Palmer dropped his hands as though it was all over. With a snort, Croot stepped in, determined to knock the impudence out of this capering, grinning young jackanape. But Palmer wasn't there. He half turned one shoulder, ducked, and was now slapping Croot's ears from behind. This went on for seventeen rounds, and Croot just couldn't find an answer, as he was outspeeded, outclassed and finally stopped.

This one fight made Palmer a King of the Ring. The next morning the whole of London was talking about the Clown who had become a Champ.

Immediately he was named the "Box of Tricks" and that name stuck to him until the end of his career. Croot had little luck after this, and four years later he was knocked out in 19 rounds at the N.S.C. by Jim Barry of Chicago. He was in such bad shape that he was removed to hospital, and died a few days later without recovering consciousness. There was such an outcry over this tragedy that proceedings followed at Bow Street police court, but all concerned in the fight were exonerated.

The Pedlar had stepped from obscurity to the dazzling spotlight of success and he accepted fame and fortune eagerly with both hands and that impudent grin. Two years later he won the British bantamweight title (then 8st. 4lbs. compared with 8st. 6lbs. to-day) beating the brilliant Birmingham bantamweight champion, Billy Plimmer in 14 rounds. An astonishing victory because Plimmer, with one minor exception, was unbeaten after five years campaigning in American rings where he had had the better of a bout with the famous Negro George Dixon, known as "Little Chocolate."

In the following year, 1896, the Pedlar went to America and although the Yankees have little time for small fighters who

76

can't punch they were astounded by the skill he displayed in holding George Dixon to a draw.

He was still unbeaten in the autumn of 1897 when two tough little Irish-American brothers—Dave and Spike Sullivan— landed in England in search of some golden sovereigns. They were a fine combination. Spike gave Jabez White, of Birmingham, holder of the British lightweight crown a hard battle at the N.S.C. And Dave fought a rugged contest with Palmer.

Dave, who packed a punch like a mule's kick, had put America's classiest bantams on their backs. As usual the little Cockney was quite undismayed by Sullivan's terrifying reputation. Pale and perkily alert he was the calmest man in the National Sporting Club when he slipped under the ropes for the most important fight of his career.

In striking contrast to the Canning Town lad's pallor and broadly evident grin, was the Yankee's mahogany tan and grimly serious expression. Dave fought in typical American fashion. He came out punching from the first bell. For round after round he gave a creditable imitation of a human cyclone, but it did him little good, because Palmer was never around, and the American spent the evening punishing thin air.

Sullivan was game. Right up to the last round he waded in as his brother Spike implored him to knockout Palmer. But he might just as well have tried to hit the moon. The Pedlar was at his best. He was a ring-ghost. In fact, the only clue Sullivan had that the London boy was in the same ring with him was when a light but peppery left would tap his nose or brush his cheek.

When the last gong sounded, Dave's lips were swollen his eyes puffed, and he was clearly outpointed, but because he had been on the attack for fifteen rounds he could not believe he had not won, and he broke down and cried in the ring when Palmer was declared the winner.

He had met the Pedlar at the zenith of his brilliant ring career. So impressed were the London boy's closest followers that they now presented him with a diamond-studded belt valued at more than £1,000. Some of the boys "borrowed" his belt. They returned it too, but some time later when Palmer had it valued he unhappily learned they had replaced the diamonds with cut glass stones.

The Londoner's first defeat came in 1899 when he returned to America to tackle Terrible Terry McGovern for the world bantamweight title. Charles Blacklock, a wealthy patron of boxing, paid all of the Pedlar's expenses, and accompanied him on the journey along with "Peggy" Bettinson.

But it proved a disastrous trip. McGovern, a wicked puncher, who had scored 12 knockout victories that year, caught the Pedlar with a smashing right hander in the first couple of minutes of this title bout at Tuckahoe, New York, and poor Pedlar became his thirteenth knockout victim before he had had time to settle down.

For the first time his amazing speed and his uncanny skill failed him, and he didn't remember a thing. He had gone out like a light. It proved to be the Pedlar's Waterloo, because although he continued fighting for twelve more years he was never quite the same again.

Two years after he had lost to McGovern, he met Harry Harris of Chicago at the Club for the world bantam title and a purse of £650. McGovern had given up the bantam crown to tackle the featherweights. Harris stood 5 ft. $7\frac{1}{2}$ in.—$4\frac{1}{2}$ in. taller than Palmer.

The Londoner had him on the canvas in the third round, but Harris later floored the Pedlar four times, and went on to win one of the finest bouts seen in the club.

The big flaw in Palmer's make-up was his lack of a devastating punch. While he was fast and uncanny in skill he more than matched his opponent but as his reflexes began to slow he was unable to keep out big hitters.

It was his lack of a punch and the fact that he was slowing down in 1904 that caused his defeat by Ben Jordan, the British featherweight champion, who came from the tannery district of Bermondsey.

Incidentally, it was Jordan who was responsible for the banning of the kidney punch in this country. He used to be a strong body puncher, and after he had knocked out Harry Greenfield with a kidney blow, the punch was made illegal in England.

Jordan, like so many other Bermondsey fighters who became champions, began with six rounds at the Bermondsey School of Arms—a high-faluting name for a ring pitched under one of the railway arches, known as the Five Hundred Arches, which lead to London Bridge.

For sixpence the spectators could watch a dozen bouts. When the money ran out the boxers on the tail-end of the programme used to wander among the crowd, cap in hand, for "nobbings" and those spectators who had spent their last coppers would usually throw a screw of shag into the caps which in those days was worth fourpence.

In 1905, the Pedlar dropped his bantam crown to up-and-coming Joe Bowker in 12 rounds. And the bottom began to fall from his kingdom of milk and honey. Like so many other Kings of the Ring he was unprepared for the rainy day. It had been easy-come and easy-go. He had always shadowed the race-tracks, and much of his cash was spent on them, but he never gave up trying to find a winner and was still seen at certain tracks in the last year or two of his life.

It was through racing that he became involved in the greatest tragedy of his life. On an Epsom train in 1907 he got into a fight with another race-goer. Palmer lost his temper, struck several blows and knocked the man unconscious. To Pedlar's horror his victim never recovered, and he was arrested for murder. In the trial at Guildford the charge was reduced to manslaughter, but he was sentenced to five years' penal servitude.

And so a curtain fell and darkened the life of the "Box of Tricks." He tried to come back at Hoxton Baths late in 1911 when he was 35 but was knocked out in 10 rounds by Darkey Haley. For six rounds he shaped up like the boy who had dazzled the onlookers against Walter Croot 18 years earlier. At the art of boxing he was just as much Haley's master as he had been Croot's, but the years between had told their inevitable tale, and the younger man moved in as the Pedlar began to wind down, and when he was finally knocked out in the 10th round a lump rose in the throat of many a ringsider.

He continued boxing throughout 1912 and revenged his defeat by Darkey Haley with a 6 round decision. He also beat Alec Lambert, George Moore, Private Walton, and Sam Russell but was beaten by Jim Lloyd and Digger Stanley.

In 1919 when nearly 43 he tackled Jim Driscoll, also past his best, but Peerless Jim beat him in 4 rounds. His last appearance was in a 3 round exhibition with Jimmy Wilde in 1922, and, believe me, what a wonderful exhibition of skill we were treated to.

As I told you, in his later years Palmer maintained he had earned £100,000 and that he had given most of it away. I would estimate his ring fortune around £25,000, but I agree most of this was either given or frittered away. He had a backer . . . a well-known bookmaker named Alf Snelling, and when Palmer had earned an estimated £1,200, Snelling advised him to put the money in the safe keeping of a bank. He couldn't understand the system of cheques, and when the "boys" realised this they used to stop the dapper little Cockney in the streets and say: "Lend us a tenner, Pedlar." A cheque duly changed hands (they had been previously signed for Palmer by Snelling). And in surprisingly quick time, Palmer had a request to call on the bank manager, who explained: "I regret to inform you, Mr. Palmer, that you have an overdraft."

"What's that?" snapped back the little boxer.

"I am afraid it means, Mr. Palmer, that you owe the bank money" explained the manager.

"Don't be silly" replied Palmer waving his cheque book. "How can I be broke when I've got all these cheques left?"

Palmer always had a mischievous trait in his make-up. He was training in the country for one important fight at the N.S.C.

and his handler, Joe Palmer, a prominent professional runner was concerned because the Pedlar instead of reducing to 8st. 4lb. was putting on weight. The more so because he used to accompany the boxer in his roadwork . . . well not quite.

There was a hill to be climbed every morning and the Pedlar with his usual cocky assurance used to say: "All right, Joe. You take it easy, I'll wait for you over the top." Then one morning the trainer suddenly solved the situation. He let the boxer go over the top as usual and then sprinting speedily caught up to find him sitting outside a pub with a pewter pot of beer to his lips. Pedlar had made an arrangement with the publican to have a pint ready every morning.

Another time, I met Palmer in Fleet Street. He was in merry mood. "Where are you going?" I said. "To see the beak at Mansion House" he replied cheerfully. "I'm up for clouting a bloke who insulted me. The boys collected a fiver last night. Forty bob fine and three quid for the old Pedlar." He rubbed his hands and chuckled. Later that afternoon the tape machine was recording that Palmer had been given a prison sentence!

There was, of course, the time when Pedlar and Joe Palmer had a difference of opinion and the boxer sought revenge. Joe laughed when he told me the story. "I was a keen gardener and grew some grand dahlias and chrysanthemums. Well, Pedlar, snooping round, discovered I was away so he brought round a billygoat and put him among my prize flowers. You can guess what was the result. "

The Pedlar remained the chirpy little Cockney with the bowler hat and choker at Brighton where he lived for years. It took a deadly opponent like pneumonia to finally knock him out at the age of 72. He had nothing left of the money he had earned in some 400 fights, but his widow was left a comfortable little house.

And so yet another artiste of the old school passed, but his name will remain immortal as long as boxing is talked, for I rate Pedlar Palmer with the Australian boxing marvel "Young Griffo" as the fastest and trickiest boxer of all time.

CHAPTER VIII

"IF I HAD MY EYES, I'D CRY!"

TIME HAD CEASED to be important for the blind old Negro, whose thinning grey kinky hair rested on his scalp like blobs of discoloured cotton wool, because he knew he was never going any place. Day after day, year after year, he had lounged on his bed in one of Harlem's many cheap apartment rooms on 139th Street, staring at the darkness and listening to the efforts of a dilapidated radio, the only companion he had left in this world. Without it, life would have been silent as well as dark for Sam Langford, the once famous Boston Tar Baby, who had become a forgotten and lonely old man, just able to keep body and soul together thanks to the local Relief Officer.

Then one cold January day in 1944 boxing's forgotten man was found again, and life has since been a little more tolerable for the man who weighed a little over 11 stone but who executed the greatest heavyweights of his day . . . a pugilist who goes down in my ratings as the most remarkable fighter never to win a title.

Langford who stood only 5 ft. 6½ inches never scaled more than a middleweight. He fought all the great fighters from light-weight to heavyweight. At 17 he outpointed the famed coloured lightweight champion Joe Gans, and at 20 he lost a points decision to Jack Johnson. In twenty-three years he took part in 640 bouts—mostly against men three and four stone heavier and only on a few occasions did he really let himself go. Like Sam McVey and Joe Jeannette, whom he fought many times, had he exerted himself more frequently he would have run out of opponents, and deprived himself of a living. And, more remarkable still, his left eye had been damaged from boyhood and in the last seven years of his fighting life the old Boston Tar Baby fought practically blind in both eyes.

It was while lying on the bed in Harlem that a New York sports columnist named Al Laney, who had spent two weeks inquiring in bars, grills, cigar stores, newspaper stands and drug-stores for a trace of the Boston Tar Baby, walked in, his object at last achieved.

Laney wrote a column about the plight of boxing's forgotten man. Few of the hundreds the reporter had spoken to had a clue as to Langford's whereabouts. Few seemed to care. At least a dozen assured him old Sam had died years before. Yet if human nature is fickle, it is also warm at the roots, for, with the story printed, thousands of boxing fans who had never even seen Langford, sent their cheques so that £2,500 was quickly raised and a Sam Langford Fund was started so that the blind old man could spend the rest of his days—not in luxury—but in comfort and with dignity.

Old Sam, touched by the thousands of letters from unknown writers, drawled: "This just proves what I always believed. Most folk is good folk. I been cheated by whites and coloured in my day, but that few don't count. If I had my eyes back, I'd cry."

I, too, find a lump rising in my throat as I think of the heavy-shouldered sightless old man of 66, now weighing nearly 17 stone who a few months back "went home" to Boston to end his days in a small hotel paid for from the small interest on the Fund.

It seems but yesterday that with Frank Bradley, an old-time sports writer, I chartered a launch to meet the Boston Tar Baby aboard the liner off Liverpool when he first came to England forty-five years ago. Langford was then unknown in England, but "Peggy" Bettinson had been tipped off about the ability of the Negro bound for England to box at the old Liverpool Gymnastic Club. "Peggy" wanted to use Langford at the N.S.C. and asked Bradley and myself to go to Liverpool to try and persuade the American party to change their minds and fight in London.

What a shock I had that morning I first set my eyes on Langford. Newspapers in those days only gave an odd paragraph to big fights taking place in America. All I knew was that this coloured fighter from Boston had given Jack Johnson a great fight. I had pictured a gargantuan Negro as big as Johnson himself. And what did I see? A little man. At least that was my first impression. But a second glance told me that he was, in fact a colossal man—a kind of Mister Five-by-Five, for the width of his tremendous shoulders—the widest pair I have ever seen—could not have been many inches short of his total height. His chest was deep and barrel-like, and his extraordinary gorilla-like arms hung loosely at his side so that the tips of his fingers drooped below his knees. Exaggerating this massive frame was a loud check suit hanging loosely in American style that would have been the envy of any bookmaker. Yet holding up this tremendous body were the short stocky legs of a lightweight. He was like something straight from the Jungle.

That was the torso of the most extraordinary fighter I ever met. Now picture his shining face—just like polished ebony beneath a nut-brown bowler hat. A flat nose spread across it, with white flashing teeth and a large mouth which mashed a black cigar and intermittently puffed out smoke and loud guffaws of laughter which earned him the nickname of Old Ho Ho.

His real manager Joe Woodman was not with the party but had sent over as his representative Jim McQuillan and Al Delmont, the Italian-American bantamweight. Frank Bradley talked McQuillan into changing his mind and it was agreed Langford's English début would be made at the National Sporting Club, but having arrived ashore neither Bradley nor I had sufficient ready cash to pay the fares to London and there were seven of us temporarily stranded until "Peggy" Bettinson wired £20 in response to our S.O.S.

Langford's arrival in Town caused a stir. Coloured folk were an unusual sight 45 years ago, and in Covent Garden the market porters stopped work as though they had set their eyes on a man from Mars. Behind us was a procession of delighted youngsters who danced and sang lustily: "I see you've got your old brown hat on!" Sam didn't mind a bit. He turned to them, lifted his famous bowler and flashed white teeth in a friendly smile.

One of the greatest difficulties was to keep him on the pavement. He kept stepping into the road when anyone approached, and was astonished when I eventually told him it was not necessary. "Where I comes from," said Langford, "coloured folk who don't make way for whites get themselves pushed off the side-walks."

Langford's first fight was against Tiger "James" Smith, a "southpaw" from Merthyr Tydvil. Smith, who sported a long and fierce-looking moustache, had taken part in many bouts in India where he served with the Army, but he was really a middleweight, and stood half an inch shorter than Langford.

The Negro trained at Stonebridge Park, and when a photographer arrived for a picture, Sam had a little joke of his own, posing as a "southpaw" with right foot and fist forward. I was with Langford the day Frank Craig, the old "Coffee Cooler," arrived at the camp. The Boston Tar Baby had been tipped off that Craig had been sent by the Smith camp to watch the "unknown" American, so he got Jim McQuillan to persuade Craig to have three rounds with him. Langford hit Craig so hard, that the Coffee Cooler didn't come up for the third round.

Tiger Smith didn't do much better. He was bubbling with confidence at the start, but Sam, knowing he could eat the so-called Tiger, shuffled along for two rounds until McQuillan had made a few bets with the Welsh "southpaw's" supporters. Once the money was down, Langford, although not going full out, showed enough to let us know he was a super fighter. One right hand was smashed to Smith's cheek splitting it to the bone. Then Langford began to warm up and, moving with the natural rhythm of the Negro, advanced opening up those massive shoulders and began to cut Smith to pieces. The Tiger, long since tamed, was completely outclassed. All he possessed was wonderful courage, but even he must have been relieved when, in the fourth round, the referee called out: "That's enough. Stop boxing."

As before the fight, Langford slipped out of the Club and took a stroll round Covent Garden puffing away at one of his beloved black cigars. Oddly, he carried a birth-mark, the perfect replica of a cigar, on his thigh. When I questioned him about it he explained: "There ain't nuthin' strange about that, boss. Before and after I was born my mammy smoked these heah cigars."

Two months later Langford was matched with Geoff Thorne, who, boxing under his correct name G. L. Townsend, had won the A.B.A. heavyweight title in 1897-98. This tall fellow with red hair was a good boxer, but stepped out of his class when he fought Langford, who flattened him in one round.

The Tar Baby went home after this, but returned in the spring of 1909 with his real manager Joe Woodman to tackle William Iron Hague, the Yorkshireman who, a month earlier, had taken the British heavyweight title from Gunner Jim Moir. Hague was not really a match for Langford, but he had the satisfaction of dropping the Negro in the fourth round with a smashing right hander which landed flush on Sam's left ear. The force of the blow caused the Tar Baby to turn a catherine wheel in the ring. He was rubbing his ear as he got to his feet—it later developed into a small cauliflower—and then, crash! A bone-breaking right hook landed on the British champion's chin. He went down as though coshed.

I have a clear picture of the scene at the N.S.C. Langford still rubbing his ear is leaning back lazily on the ropes and looking carelessly down at the twitching form of Iron Bill. He grins as he glances to Hague's corner where the excited seconds are screaming: "Get up, Iron! Get up, Bill!" Then leaning over the ropes he drawls almost confidentially:

"Say, boys. He ain't gonna get up. That baby's out for keeps." Sam was right.

Lord Lonsdale, in tails, white waistcoat, long cigar and gardenia in coat lapel, was one of the first to congratulate Langford on his victory. Britain's most famous sportsman was fond of coloured boxers, having claimed to have discovered the great Peter Jackson in a competition in San Francisco.

Certainly, Jackson trained at his lordship's estate, Barley Thorpe, Oakham, as did another brilliant coloured fighter, George Dixon, world bantam and featherweight champion. But I think Lord Lonsdale was carried away when he used to claim he himself had once knocked out the mighty John L. Sullivan . . . a story that was always met with a smile by Americans.

Langford's only other fight in England was against the Australian bushman Bill Lang at Olympia in 1911 and was staged by the late Hugh D. McIntosh, who had promoted the Jack Johnson-Tommy Burns world heavyweight championship in Sydney three years earlier.

McIntosh, who began working in a restaurant but later became a wealthy newspaper magnate and afterwards ran a chain of milk-bars in London, was the first promoter in Britain to lift boxing from the atmosphere of sawdust and kerosene lamps into the magnificence we know to-day.

McIntosh really believed he had found in his six-foot, fourteen-stone fellow countryman a world beater and began a build-up campaign in London. Lang had certainly impressed with a workmanlike job by knocking out Californian Jack Burns on his first appearance here.

The promoter announced a £3,500 purse for the Langford-Lang slam—a tremendous figure for those days. Hugh D. was a master of ballyhoo. His "Black v. White" bout appealed to Mayfair, and most ringsiders were in full evening dress, while it was the first time I recall well-dressed women attending boxing in large numbers. McIntosh had even succeeded in knocking the hard-boiled boxing writers groggy.

He introduced a novelty in the shape of a set of all-white boxing gloves. He had stewards in short white linen coats and

87

brass buttons. At one end of the arena a full military band played the gladiators into the ring. Jimmy Britt, the former American lightweight, dolled up in tails, was the M.C. It was a triumph of organisation.

McIntosh considered Langford would be a cinch for his gigantic bushranger. Lang certainly had every physical advantage. He was 7½ inches taller than the Negro and more than two stone heavier. When they came to the centre of the ring it looked as though a ridiculous match had been made. The lanky bushman towered over the gorilla-like Langford.

The Tar Baby gave a lazy little shuffle as he shook hands and listened to the referee's instructions, but he wasn't listless once the gong sounded and he moved into action as ferocious as a bull-dog. Lang was game. Dead game, but that was all. Again we saw legalised slaughter from Langford as he cut the Australian to ribbons.

McIntosh could not believe his eyes. As blood poured from cuts above the Australian's eyes and from his nose, the promoter leaned over the press seats and attempted to reassure himself: "Don't take any notice of the blood, Jimmy" he said, "Lang always bleeds when hit. He'll get going in a couple of rounds."

Lang never got going that night. He spent the greater part of each round bent almost double doing his best to avoid the murderous punches that Sam's long arms were swinging and smashing home from all angles. The Tar Baby's white gloves were now red with blood—Lang's blood. Once rising after a count of 7, the Australian managed to catch Langford with a wild right hook on the chin.

The Tar Baby flashed white teeth in a grin . . . an ugly frightening grin. Then he crouched even lower and the glint in his eye forecast trouble for Lang. It was the same glint he had shown when Iron Hague had given him his cauliflower ear shortly before Iron was poleaxed, and Sam had leaned against the ropes and drawled: "He ain't gonna get up. That baby's out for keeps."

Langford belted him and cut him still more. To Lang's

credit he refused to stay down, but he lost his head completely. The Negro had missed with a right and slipped to one knee. The desperate Aussie went after him and threw a wild punch for which Eugene Corri rightly disqualified him. A disappointing ending, but it made no difference for Lang never had a chance of beating the squat man who had few masters in any part of the world.

Great as he was, Langford never earned big money. Of his 640 bouts he reckoned he received less than £250 for five hundred of them. Like all the leading Negros before Joe Louis—Jack Johnson excepted—Langford had to pull his punches in many fights.

He took part in dozens of bouts with Sam McVey and Joe Jeannette, but never was given a crack at the world title. He had only the one fight with Jack Johnson at Chelsea, Massachusetts, but that was three years before Johnson won the title. Each boxer took a count in that contest. Langford chased Johnson through America, Britain, France and Australia. Manager Joe Woodman publicly challenged Johnson, but they could never get Lil' Arthur to give Sam a second chance. This has been taken as meaning that Johnson feared Sam. I can't believe that, but what a great championship battle it would have been.

Langford's blindness was not caused directly by boxing. As a boy, whilst white-washing a cook-house in Boston, a pail of lime fell over him and went into his eyes. He didn't pay attention to it, and as a result his left eye began to deteriorate.

When he fought Fred Fulton in 1917 a right-hand punch blinded him. He went to hospital next day, and was told it was a miracle he hadn't lost his sight ten years before. The cord of the optic nerve was almost burned off. A cataract grew over the other eye, and so one of the great kings of the ring joined the legion of the sightless.

Yet before he retired at 38 he won fights practically blind in Mexico, Panama and California. Once in Mexico City in an afternoon contest the sun was so glaring that Sam couldn't see a thing. His Spanish opponent jabbed him twice in the first round, and the groping Langford instinctively let fly with his famous right hook. If it had missed Sam would never have found his opponent again, but it landed and the Spaniard was out.

There must have been many stories told about Sam's great sense of humour, but the tale I liked best occurred before the Tiger Smith fight at the N.S.C. when a meeting was held to decide who should referee. Throughout the argument Sam sat in a corner blissfully unconcerned.

Then Lord Lonsdale finally turned to him and courteously inquired: "How about you, Mr. Langford? What is your attitude towards the proposed referee?"

Sam gave one of his broadest smiles: "Chief, you jess name any referee you like. Ah always takes ma own right along with me."

"Your own referee?" inquired Lord Lonsdale.

Sam held up his right fist and laughed: "Chief, here he is. There ain't never been an argument after he's given his decision."

CHAPTER IX

GREATEST FIGHTER WHO NEVER WON A TITLE

"You're Wrong, Jimmy Butler" snapped the grey-haired little man with the nose too large for the sallow face which had grown smaller as the result of sunken cheeks. And smacking his right fist down on one of the tables of Jack Dempsey's Broadway Restaurant added, as though a proved fact and not just voicing an opinion, "The roughest, toughest and greatest son of a gun you people ever shipped to the States was Owen Moran of Birmingham."

I raised my eyebrows for the speaker was Abe Attell, now 69, regarded as one of America's immortal champions. Nodding assent were Dumb Dan Morgan and Francis Albertini, last of the old-timers whose opinions must always be respected by anybody who knows anything about fighting.

Only a few seconds earlier as we sat sipping coffee at Dempsey's, Albertini had asked me to name the greatest boxer Britain had ever sent to America and, knowing my audience to consist of experts, I had paused before replying: "It must be a toss up between Jimmy Wilde, Jim Driscoll, Ted Kid Lewis, Freddy Welsh and Matt Wells—always leaving aside old Bob Fitzsimmons who had left England as a child."

As Attell made his sweeping statement I recalled the late Jimmy Johnston, who had handled the cream of British champions in the United States, had once described Moran to me as "the world's greatest fighting man for his inches."

Remarkable that American old-timers regard the tough little Birmingham scrapper as Britain's greatest boxing ambassador when he won neither a world nor British title. Perhaps it was because Moran was a fighter after their own hearts. A tearaway terrier who wasn't afraid of any Great Dane as he proved when hammering out the ex-lightweight champion of the world Battling Nelson from Denmark.

And they remember his five great battles with Attell—two drawn for the world featherweight title in Abe's home town, San Francisco, and three bitter "No Decision" bouts.

I cannot agree Moran was greater than, say, Wilde or Driscoll, but I hasten to add I consider him in the top six of our best-ever fighters.

There has never been a fiercer fighter inside or outside the ring than this Birmingham-born bantam cock, who stood 5ft. 3ins., never scaled more than 8st. 4lbs., but had broad shoulders, a powerful aggressive chin and the clearest of pale blue eyes. In fact, Nature was pretty generous to Owen Moran, giving him most of the treasured gifts a man can have . . . everything barring one important asset—a sense of humour. For Owen was a grim-faced young man who had never learned to laugh as a child, and who grew up with those melancholy crystal-clear eyes, and a determination that nobody on two legs would ever put one over him.

He was fearless, but while courage is admired, I must add that Moran took himself and life too seriously. He had a heart of gold, yet to pull his leg was risking a challenge to a duel, for the little man from Birmingham would just as soon hit you on the chin as look at you if he thought you were trying to crack a joke at his expense. And he wasn't interested whether you stood eye to eye with him or whether you were 6ft. 3ins. and 14 stone.

Moran, like Jimmy Wilde, didn't know how to pull a punch. He was born to fight and to fight ruthlessly whether on the streets of Birmingham where he grew up or in Harry Cullis's booth which toured the Midlands. He couldn't even hold back in an exhibition. At one of "Peggy" Bettinson's annual benefits at the National Sporting Club, Moran sparred exhibition with Tom Ringer, amateur bantam and feather-weight champion.

The Lynn boxer was a splendid champion, and gave Moran plenty of trouble. The Birmingham battler was the last man in the world to allow an amateur to make a fool of him in front of N.S.C. members, and he moved in on Ringer as though he himself was fighting for dear life. It ceased to be an exhibition, but a survival of the fittest. The hard-hitting Moran, so intent on proving himself the better man, once swung round on his heels, and landed a pivot punch smack on Ringer's mouth—an unexpected blow for an exhibition.

Afterwards, I strolled over the old Waterloo Bridge to catch a tram with Matt Wells and Ringer. Tom was in pain and complained: "Every tooth in my head feels loose." Wells examined Ringer's mouth and was so worried that they turned back over the bridge and made for the casualty ward of Charing Cross Hospital.

The little warrior who was born to fight couldn't even contain himself when describing one of his fights. I know that to my cost. It was soon after his return from America in my little office off Fleet Street that Moran, as excited as a schoolboy, was relating to me just how he had knocked out Nelson.

One minute he was shadow boxing and dancing on his toes. Suddenly I thought the roof had caved in on me. I felt dizzy, bemused and quite sick as bright lights flickered before my eyes. Two or three Owen Morans weaved in front of me like drunken ghosts. Yet although a pain was darting through my head I recall being impressed by a most unusual sight. Moran was smiling. Yes, there was no mistaking he was grinning even though half apologetically.

In his enthusiasm to show me how he had flattened Nelson he had let a punch go and it had half caught me on the chin.

"I'm sorry, Jimmy," he gasped. "I didn't realise I was so near to you when I let that one go, but good for you, boy, you took it. Battling Nelson went out like a snuffed candle."

I felt my jaw tenderly, and grated my teeth to make sure none

93

of them were missing. I was grateful that Moran had only half caught me. I never met Owen Moran again without ducking jocularly before we shook hands. The little incident did much to cement a great friendship between us, and to the end of his days Moran always maintained that his knockout victory over the Durable Dane, famed for his iron jaw, was his greatest.

Moran's aggressive nature had him in plenty of trouble outside the ring. After beating Al Delmont, the highly-rated Italian-American, over 20 rounds at the N.S.C. he was invited to box in America under the management of Charlie Harvey and Jimmy Johnston. In his own grim way he arrived in New York determined the wise guys would not take the "shine" out of him. He was looking for trouble from the moment he set foot on American soil, and seeing a coloured porter at the quayside he snapped: "See here, Nigger, pick up my bags." The porter ignored Moran's ill-mannered command, and the Birmingham fighter's blood was up. "A fresh coon, eh?" he he jeered and half running towards the Negro, smashed home a punch on the chin, knocking the porter cold.

He also hated New York cops. "They take me for some soft Limey," he used to complain, and carried the war into their camp by deliberately seeking information, and picking quarrels with them if he didn't like the tone of their answers. The late Charlie Harvey, who brought Moran to America, was always dipping into his pocket to get the boy from Brum out of trouble with the police. Owen was fearless but bull-headed enough to think he could declare war on the New York City Police—and win!

Before he fought Matt Wells in Sydney, whilst weighing-in, Owen suddenly spotted a man against whom he carried a grudge. He jumped off the platform and darted through the door into George Street, the main thoroughfare in Sydney, with only a towel tucked round his mid-section. He was brought back to the weigh-in ceremony still breathing lurid threats against his enemy.

He spent five years in America between 1908 and 1913

94

fighting every type of champion from foxy stylists like Abe Attell and accomplished Packy McFarland, to smashing two-fisted, non-stop battlers such as Nelson and Ad Wolgast, both ex-world champions. And each he played at his own game for he knew enough of the science of boxing to hold his own with a master like McFarland and sufficient tricks of the trade to match the brilliance of Attell, but he was happiest of all against the rugged, cyclonic methods of Nelson.

Moran was never an angel, but he was a good-hearted fellow until he hit the bottle. Then he became impossible.

One day he arrived at Los Angeles after one of his drinking bouts, and began immediately to pick a quarrel in a hotel lobby with Jimmy Johnston, then a young man and a tough scrapper himself. Johnston was on his way to a dinner and was wearing a tuxedo. "What are yer all dressed up for, Monk?" sneered Moran.

Johnston, himself quick tempered, took it for awhile, but becoming angry snarled back: "Why don't you shut that big Limey mouth of yours or I'll pin back those plastered ears."

Moran, drunk or sober, could not resist a challenge like this. He swung a left and a right which clipped Jimmy's chin, and quickly Johnston, who had been born fighting on New York's East Side, was retaliating.

He grabbed Moran by his coat lapels, butted him several times with his head which had the British fighter, already unsteady on his feet, reeling and groggy. Moran retaliated, and Johnston's face was soon smothered in blood.

It was an ugly rough-house brawl. Both men fought like crazy tigers, as excited passers-by ran into the lobby from the side-walks.

Johnston was getting the worst of it, until he tripped up Moran and, in an uncontrollable temper, sprang on to him, banging the boxer's head back and forward on the hotel floor. A friend of the enraged manager dragged him off the boxer, and certainly saved Moran's life.

Owen was rushed to hospital unconscious, and was treated

for a broken jaw, concussion, a fractured hand, cut eyes, ripped ears and a score of cuts and bruises. Johnston staggered to a friend's room in the hotel, his evening dress torn to shreds, blood pouring from his head, both eyes blackened and handfuls of hair missing. A doctor bandaged him up.

Johnston returned to New York, but Moran went from 'Frisco to Australia for some contests, but leaving plenty of messages for Johnston vowing vengeance. Months later Moran returned to San Francisco and wired Charlie Harvey he was on his way to New York.

Harvey telephoned Johnston: "Listen, Jimmy, Owen Moran is on his way to New York. Get out of Town till he quietens down. We don't want any more trouble."

But Johnston, like Moran, was fearless and refused to leave although he had heard all about Moran's sworn vengeance. He arrived at the office he shared with Harvey, prepared to produce the velvet glove—or the iron fist if Moran wanted it that way.

But even Jimmy was shaken when Moran arrived and shouted out: "Hullo, Monk, old boy." Later over a meal, Moran took Jimmy aside and said: "Let bygones be bygones, Jimmy. I know I go daffy when I drink too much, but I want to be your friend." They shook hands on it.

That was the nice side of Owen Moran. Naturally aggressive, impossible in drink, but always fair. His sportsmanship was terrific, for in the States he was handed out many a raw deal by home-town decisions, including two drawn bouts with Attell for the world featherweight title, but he took them all philosophically, seldom complaining, only asking for another chance to prove himself the better man.

Moran was first spotted in Harry Cullis's booth by my old colleague, Captain Harry Cleveland, who recommended him for a fight at the N.S.C. He never looked back, and one of the first to become acquainted with his knockout punch was Charlie Smirke, father of the famed jockey. It would be true to say he almost began fighting in championship class because

Vive la France! Poor old Joe! Another British heavyweight hope bites the dust. Georges Carpentier of France flattens Joe Beckett, the British champion, for the second time in a matter of seconds, on October 1, 1923.

Owch! The Rock packs a Wallop. Jersey Joe Walcott's head seems to be made of rubber as a right-hander from Rocky Marciano shatters Jersey Joe. A few seconds later Walcott is down and out after having outpointed Rocky for 13 rounds. This one big punch gained the world heavyweight title on September 23, 1952.

he was only 16 when he went 20 rounds with Digger Stanley. He lost again to the Digger over 15 rounds three years later, but gained his revenge in a third bout over 20 rounds.

Owen's No. 1 rival was Peerless Jim Driscoll. He tried everything to get a match with Driscoll, but the pity of it was that they never stepped into the ring together until both were past their best in 1913 when they boxed a 20-rounds draw. They had both been under the Harvey-Johnston management in America, but because of the Birmingham lad's threats of what he would do to Driscoll, they had to be trained in separate gyms!

Moran's greatest triumph was over Battling Nelson on November 26, 1910. The knocking out of the Durable Dane in 11 rounds at San Francisco was a boxing bombshell which shook American fight fans from Coast to Coast. Nelson had for fourteen years been taking on all the crack lightweights with only one previous knockout registered against him, and this only nine months earlier when he had lost his world lightweight crown to Ad Wolgast, the German-American, when the referee awarded Wolgast the fight on a k.o. in the 40th round.

Owen licked Nelson by sheer toughness and courage. The Dane was 28, but heavier and more experienced than Moran, and you could have got 1,000-1 odds against the little Brum, who was only a big bantam, scoring a knockout.

When the grim-faced Midlander began wading into the Danish battering-ram, swapping punch for punch, the fight already looked as good as over, for the few who had dared fight Nelson at his own game had always been carried to their corners.

For round after round they fought like demons. Neither man prided himself on science. They just exchanged shattering blows, and the blood spurted across the ring. They looked a sorry couple, but any sympathy would have been wasted for both these great pugilists were happiest when the blood was flowing and each knew there could not be such a thing as surrender. The winner would have to knock his opponent completely senseless.

Nelson had realised by the eighth round that this cheeky little fellow from England was a super fighter with strength, stamina and speed that could not be mastered. He was fighting even more desperately than in those epic battles he had against the old Negro master, Joe Gans.

Moran became stronger as the Durable Dane discovered he was durable no longer. He was fading, but nobody had expected to see the English boy come out for the eleventh round and with a vicious right swing drop Nelson like a log.

Seven months later Moran tackled Ad Wolgast, who was still lightweight champion of the world, at San Francisco. The Birmingham fighter was giving away plenty of weight against a world champion, and was wading in with both hands taking terrific punishment himself. Bravely Moran gave and took for thirteen rounds until the Michigan Bear-Cat sank a wicked right swing into Owen's body. Moran went down in terrible pain, claiming he was fouled. A photograph showed him twisted on the canvas with both gloves gripping his groin.

Moran was never the same fighter again. He returned to England a year later to tackle Driscoll at the National Sporting Club, but the spark had gone out of both these great fighters, and they fought a dull 20-rounds draw.

It was odd that Moran who fought the best fighters in Britain and America over 15 years should always fail in a title fight. As a 19-year-old bantam he could not succeed in lifting the crown from the brilliant Salford champion, Joe Bowker. His featherweight bid against Driscoll was drawn when he was 28, and approaching 31 he tried again but was disqualified against the Welsh featherweight Llew Edwards.

Two of his five bouts with Abe Attell were for the world featherweight title in Abe's home town, San Francisco, in 1908 and he failed. The first ended in a 25-rounds draw and the second, eight months later, was also drawn over 23 rounds.

After Owen retired in 1916, he was often seen on the race-tracks and was fortunate in having a good friend in Ted Salmon, one-time Birmingham promoter, who looked after him in his darker days.

A few years ago I was in Birmingham with Lee Savold and my son Frank. A little man who looked very ill began arguing about boxing. He was a little cantankerous but knowledgeable, and I was shocked when I realised it was the shadow of Owen Moran, now 64. Death stared from his protruding eyes. I, one of his oldest friends, did not introduce myself because I didn't want him to know how unrecognisable was this fading shadow of the devil-may-care I had once known, with the broad shoulders, aggressive chin and clear-blue eyes. I let him air his views without a murmur. I was glad because 3 weeks later Owen Moran, whose name was never inscribed on the roll of champions, but was without doubt one of the great performers of the British ring, was dead.

The Midlands have produced other fine fighters. From Birmingham years earlier had come truculent Charlie Mitchell, a middleweight who met John L. Sullivan and Jim Corbett. He had fought a drawn battle of 39 rounds at Chantilly, France, in 1888 with Sullivan. Mitchell wasn't afraid of any creature living and did almost as much fighting in the bars as in the ring.

There was also Jabez White, one of our most scientific champions, who I watched twice outpoint Spike Sullivan of America at the Club and who held the lightweight title of Britain until he lost it to Jack Goldswain of Bermondsey in one of the biggest surprises ever staged at the N.S.C.

Birmingham also gave us British flyweight champion Bert Kirby who had three title fights with Jackie Brown of Manchester. Their first battle at West Bromwich on October 13, 1929, took place on Sunday—the only time a British title has been contested on the Sabbath.

And there was, of course, Jack Hood, one of the classiest welterweight champions we have had. Hood, who won a Lonsdale Belt outright, also tackled our best middleweights, taking part in three championship battles with Len Harvey, losing two and drawing one.

When Hood retired he did so without a ring scar, which was a great tribute to his skill. He is still a handsome figure at 51—sometimes he acts as M.C. at a Midlands promotion—and I enjoy talking with him on my visits to the Midlands where he keeps a pub at Tamworth-in-Arden.

Birmingham has certainly provided us with some mighty pugilists—but the mightiest of them all was little Owen Moran.

CHAPTER X

THE DASHING, SLASHING, SMASHING, BASHING, CRASHING KID

THEY SAY ANYTHING can happen in the fight game. Yet after more than half a century among the resin and sawdust, I find myself puzzled that at the time of writing there is not one Jewish boxer holding a championship of the world or Britain. What, you might ask, is so surprising about this? Well, would you expect to find an England football team without an Englishman in it? This may at first sound a little exaggerated, but it is a fact that to-day world boxing is largely controlled by the descendants of Israel. They are well represented among the boxers, and also officials of every kind including promoters, matchmakers, managers, referees, seconds, timekeepers, M.C.'s, medical officers and also make up the large percentage of a big fight crowd at Harringay, White City and other big arenas. That is why I am amazed at not being able to trace a champion from among the race who, in the past, have produced some of the immortals like Benny Leonard, Abe Attell, Ted Kid Lewis, Matt Wells, Barney Ross and Jackie Kid Berg to name a few.

The Negro has made greater progress in boxing than any other race in the past fifteen or twenty years. While there is not a Hebrew champion in possession of a world title, the descendants of Shem have in the past produced a world champion at every weight from fly to heavy—seventeen in all. Here they are:—

Heavy: Max Baer (German-Scottish)
Cruiser: Battling Levinsky (American)
            Maxie Rosenbloom (American)
Middle: Ben Jeby—N.Y. Commission title (American)
            Solly Krieger—N.B.A. champion (American)

Welter:	Ted Kid Lewis
	Jackie Fields (American)
	Barney Ross (American)
Light:	Benny Leonard (American)
	Al Singer (American)
Feather:	Solly Smith
	Abe Attell (American)
	Louis Kid Kaplan (Russian)
	Benny Bass (Russian)
Bantam:	Abe Goldstein (American)
	Charley Rosenberg (American)
Fly:	Izzy Schwartz (American)

While there hasn't been a British heavyweight or flyweight champion with Jewish blood in his veins over the same period, there have been title holders in the other six divisions. I give the list:—

Heavy:	None
Cruiser:	Jack Bloomfield
Middle:	Ted Kid Lewis
Welter:	Young Joseph
	Ted Kid Lewis
	Harry Mason
Light:	Matt Wells
	Harry Mason
	Harry Mizler
	Jack Kid Berg
Feather:	Ted Kid Lewis
	Joe Fox
	Al Phillips (Won British Empire and European titles, but not British championship)
Bantam:	Joe Fox
	Johnny Brown
Fly:	None

England had one Jewish heavyweight champion—even though he scaled barely 11 stone and stood but 5ft. 7ins. I am talking of Daniel Mendoza. He was born at Aldgate and was the sixteenth heavyweight champion of England under Prize Ring Rules. Mendoza was one of the first prize fighters to demonstrate that size and strength were not the chief assets of a pugilist but that science and defensive skill could match brute force and that a David could bring down a Goliath.

Mendoza was once financed by a King of England. His long black hair cost him his fight against Gentleman Jackson, who grabbed the tresses with one hand and punched him into submission with the other. Like so many other champs who have followed him, Mendoza died a pauper at 73.

From the birth-place of Mendoza have sprung a strong band of Jewish scrappers. The old Wonderland in Whitechapel, followed by Premierland, were nurseries for their youngsters. And, in a smaller way, so was the Judean Club. Years later the East End produced the Devonshire Club in Hackney, where Jack Solomons learned his stuff that was to make him the leading promoter in Britain, if not the world. In this old arena, formerly a chapel, which was destroyed in the blitz, Jewish fight fans mainly sat downstairs and the Christians in the balcony. Many a Sunday afternoon I sat there while Jew fought Christian inside the ring, and the roar of the crowd was split in half.

One of the early stars of the East End was Young Aschel Joseph who, like Jack Solomons, was born in Petticoat Lane. Joseph took thousands of followers with him wherever he fought, and met every top-notcher from bantam to welterweight.

Other champs, or near-champs of his race, include Sam Keller Matt Wells, Jack Kid Berg, Jack Hyams, Harry Mizler, Benny Caplan, Harry Mason, Jack Bloomfield, Joe Fox, Al Phillips, Vic Herman and the two Browns—Johnny and Young Johnny.

But the top champion the London Ghetto ever produced was Ted Kid Lewis—perhaps only surpassed by America's superb Hebrew fighter Benny Leonard, who took the world lightweight title from Freddy Welsh. America raved about The Kid. He lived up to the billing the late Jimmy Johnston, who managed him in the States, gave him—the "Dashing, Slashing, Smashing, Bashing, Crashing **Kid**." James J. Corbett once declared him to be the "finest fighter for his pounds in the ring to-day."

The Kid didn't want to know much about boxing, but what a fighter and non-stop terror for twenty rounds. It is forty-three years ago since he first called on me in Fleet Street. A thin shy lad of fourteen, who twisted his small black velvet cap nervously between his fingers as he made this request: "Would you please write me up in your boxing notes, sir? I'm a fighter, and I'm going to try and win a championship."

"What is your name, lad?" I inquired, avoiding any cynical grin that might hurt the feelings of this white-faced, lean youngster who revealed nothing to suggest he had the stuff of what champions are made. I was, however, impressed by the keenness of his clear eyes which stared into mine, and told me this youth sincerely believed in everything he had told me.

"Gershon Mendeloff, sir," he replied, "but round Aldgate they call me 'The Kid'."

Later his name was to gain respect throughout Britain, Australia and America . . . not as Gershon Mendeloff, son of an East End cabinetmaker, but as Ted Kid Lewis. He received no encouragement from his father for on his first visit to me he confided that the biggest handicap to his boxing ambitions was that he dare not talk about it to his father because the serious-minded non-sporting Solomon Mendeloff was determined his boy would carry on in his shoes as cabinet-maker.

Little did he know his boy each morning visited Victoria Park at Hackney—not to study nature, but to put in strenuous road-work, and rowed on the lake not because he liked boats but to develop his chest and arms to serve him inside a boxing ring.

And occasionally he had, quite unbeknown to his father, taken part in six-round bouts in the Judean Club for sixpence and a shilling a time . . . or even a cup of tea and a slice of cake. Ted Kid Lewis was not really interested in money. He just fought for the sheer love of it.

In America he earned a fortune—estimated at half a million

dollars, but he still wasn't interested in the financial side of the fight game. True, he liked to live well. He drove high-powered cars, dressed magnificently and bought ridiculously expensive presents for his friends and even acquaintances. It was nothing unusual for The Kid to hand over presents of gold watches, diamond pins and cigarette cases. I was standing talking to him in Brighton one day when Syd Walker, the old comedian, strolled up and joined our conversation. "Boy! That's some pin you're sporting," said Syd, unable to conceal his admiration. "Did you get it in the States?"

"Yes," smiled The Kid, "there's plenty more where this one came from," and lifting the pin off himself, stuck it into Syd Walker's tie, at the same time tightening the comedian's neck-piece with a smile, and added: "It looks better on you than me, anyway, Syd!"

Another day he arrived at a West End club in a new pale-blue sports car which was admired by many. He offered it as a gift to a member of the National Sporting Club, who, in spite of The Kid's persuasive manner, simply refused to take advantage of the boxer's absurd generosity.

Like Jimmy Wilde, Georges Carpentier and other champs, Lewis was fighting regularly in his early teens. At fourteen, fifteen and sixteen he was in such demand that he had 64 bouts in 1911 and 1912 and only lost one of them—and this on a foul after 7 rounds to Con Houghton, who had won the A.B.A. featherweight crown in 1910.

His reputation had spread so much that at sixteen he was invited to box at the N.S.C. This was The Kid's big chance. Wise fistic Men of the East were raving about him. Now he could show the Wise Men of the West that he was a champ in the making. But disaster hit Lewis. His opponent, Duke Lynch of Camberwell, released a right-hander to The Kid's chin and for the first time he was counted out—and in the opening round at that!

But other champions have had to face similar set-backs early in their careers—Dempsey, Carpentier and Louis to name a few. The fact they came back after being knocked out was in itself proof of their greatness.

Lewis beat Lynch in a return bout at Blackfriars Ring in the summer of 1913, and a few months later—eighteen days before his seventeenth birthday—he won the British featherweight title, stopping Alec Lambert in 17 rounds at the N.S.C. No other British boxer has won a title at such an early age, and none ever will because the British Boxing Board of Control rules now bar a boxer under 21 taking part in a fifteen round contest. Eric Boon came closest to Kid Lewis's record when in 1938 he knocked out Dave Crowley to win the lightweight title when he was 18.

Lambert, the ex-amateur champion, was favourite to beat The Kid from the East End. Some members even declared it was a disgrace to allow the white-faced boy to attempt twenty rounds against a seasoned champ like Lambert.

But like so many of The Kid's opponents, Lambert had under-estimated the fierce determination behind those clear eyes which had warned me not to be too hasty to pack him off when, as a 14-year-old, he had "gate-crashed" Fleet Street to tell me of his ambitions three years earlier.

Like so many of his opponents Lambert had not realised that Lewis's skinny, pasty body was all steel and whipcord, while on his shoulders and forearms man-sized muscles were beginning to ripple, hinting of the punching powers that were to make him such a formidable foe.

Also The Kid was determined to make good after that first humiliating defeat by Duke Lynch at the N.S.C. when the wise-guys had scoffed and sneered: "Didn't we tell you he was a cardboard champion?" And yet another important reason. He wanted to take home a treasured Lord Lonsdale Belt just to prove to old Solomon Mendeloff that the career he had chosen against his father's wishes was not wasted. That he had won the highest honour any English boxer could achieve.

And that night The Kid was a fighting demon. Members didn't see the straight left of Driscoll or the skill of Pedlar

Palmer. Instead, they witnessed a fighting octopus. An English boy who had a natural American style without having yet travelled the length and breadth of London Town.

Yet his face, as always, wore a mask of complacency. For Lewis was the sphinx of the ring, never revealing any excitement or emotion within. Lambert wisely tried to keep the fight at long range, and to use his greater science and ring-craft to expose the rawness of this little boy from Aldgate. But how can you stop a river flowing or lightning flashing?

The East-Ender was a young tiger. From the first gong he set a breathless, furious pace, forcing Lambert backwards— yes, always backwards. The older champion wilted before this youthful dynamo who seemed to grow stronger as the rounds came.

Lambert's stamina faded and, as well as he boxed, it was all over in the 17th. The beaten champion smiled a little when I came into his dressing room. "I thought it was raining boxing gloves to-night" he said.

Lewis was still seventeen when he won the European title, beating Paul Til on a foul, and he went on to lift the welter and middleweight crowns of Great Britain, and the world's welterweight title.

After beating Til he invaded Australia and defeated top-notchers like Herb McCoy, Hughie Mehegan and the tough American Young Shugrue. From there he went to New York to begin the most successful tour any British pugilist ever made before or since in the United States.

In his fighting ferocity he equalled little Owen Moran. Charley Harvey, who handled the best British boxers in America, rated Lewis with Driscoll and Moran, as the finest of the English fighters he had watched.

The Kid's battles with Jack Britton set up an all-time record in marathon fighting between March, 1915, and February, 1921, when the pair met twenty times in all. Not only did Charlie Harvey and Jimmy Johnston swear to me that every battle between the pair was on the level, but that they were the two greatest welters of all time. So evenly were they matched that each bout was a blood-bath, and each meeting involved a battle of wits between Johnston, and Dumb Dan Morgan, famous veteran manager of Britton.

There wasn't an official welterweight champion of the world at this time, but the Americans reckoned Jack Britton was about their No.1 fighter in this division. They became impressed with Lewis after his New York début when he gave Phil Bloom a real going over in the old Madison Square Garden. The Kid also impressed against Young Jack O'Brien in Philadelphia and against Britton in New York. All these were "No Decision" bouts as many States at this time would not allow decisions to be awarded.

Dan Morgan and Jimmy Johnston then got together and decided that if they took the pair to Boston—decisions were still allowed in Massachusetts—they could clean up some cash, and get one of their fighters officially recognised as world champion. Johnston had claimed the title after Lewis had got the newspaper verdict in a "No Decision" bout against Willie Ritchie in 1915, but it wasn't until he received a decision over Britton the same year that he became recognised as official champion.

Twenty times they met in thirteen different cities. 11 bouts were without decisions, 2 were drawn, Lewis gained three verdicts and Britton four. While the Kid and Britton hammered each other inside the ring, Jimmy Johnston and Dan Morgan juggled outside, each trying to pull a stroke over the other. Such as bringing along their own referee. In the "No Decision" bouts out of town there would be a race between them to get telegraphs off to the New York papers, each giving their own account of how the fight went.

In spite of bickerings and arguments Lewis was still recognised as champion until Britton knocked him out in 9 rounds at Dayton, Ohio, on March 17, 1919.

Later that year Lewis returned to England after five years' absence and stopped Matt Wells in 12 rounds at the Albert

Hall. In 1920 he swept all British opposition before him, beating Frank Moody, Gus Platts, and taking the British welterweight title off gallant Johnny Basham who had already won outright a Lord Lonsdale Belt.

They met at Olympia in June. Basham, born at Newport in 1890, had learned his boxing while serving with the Royal Welch Fusiliers. He was a good boxer, and one of his best performances was when he won the title beating Johnny Summers nearly six years earlier.

But Basham had little chance against Lewis with The Kid's great American experience behind him, and after nine thrilling rounds the referee, in spite of Basham's protests, stopped the bout as blood poured from Johnny's mouth—a tooth having pierced the roof of his mouth.

Basham wouldn't admit Lewis was his master, and they were re-matched for the title at the Albert Hall five months later. For four rounds the smiling, stylish Basham gave Lewis a boxing lesson, but it didn't mean very much because The Kid was boring in and roughing the Newport boxer up inside. At a distance there was only one man in it—and that was Basham the boxer. But Lewis, his expressionless face not giving away his inner feelings, kept tearing in, sapping the stamina of Basham, not in the least disturbed that he was behind on points at the half-way stage.

The thirteenth round was unlucky for Basham. Lewis, now putting on pressure, split Johnny's ear with a vicious right, and the blood ran down his neck. The Kid made this his target until Basham became so concerned that he began to protect only his damaged ear. This was the signal for Lewis to open up a vicious body attack again, and Basham began to wilt. He took the first knockdown in the fifteenth round more from weakness than from Lewis's punch. For four more rounds Basham's courage astounded ringsiders, hoping he would now stay the full twenty rounds, but twice in the 19th round he was floored from heavy rights, and although on each occasion he gamely dragged himself up at 9, Eugene Corri rushed in after the second knockdown and stopped the slaughter, maintaining that gallant Johnny Basham had not beaten the count.

They met twice more. In 1921 Lewis took the middleweight crown from Basham, beating him in 12 rounds at the Albert Hall, and finally as late as 1929 when both came out of retirement to box at Hoxton Baths, and the 40-year-old Basham was stopped in three rounds.

In 1922 Lewis, afraid of nothing on two legs, gave weight, height and reach to Carpentier who had flattened our heavyweights Billy Wells and Joe Beckett and who still held the world's light-heavyweight crown. Lewis had been boxing for twelve years and was definitely past his best, but for two thrill-packed minutes the Aldgate Kid tore into the surprised Frenchman and exposed Carpentier's form as it had never been exposed by any British opponent.

Those who had expected the courageous East End middleweight to go the same way as Beckett and Wells came to their feet excitedly as Carpentier backed away. That Georges was disturbed was clear. His charm had disappeared, and he revealed his teeth in an ugly snarl. He was the apache fighting with his back to the wall, and win he must.

Lewis was still non-stop in the clinches, and Carpentier was hanging on trying to stop the fury of the East Ender and at the same time steadying himself for his lightning right hand. The referee, Joe Palmer, shouted at both boxers as he ran between them. "Stop holding!" he commanded. For once Lewis's poker-face flushed angrily, and he half turned to Palmer to protest that he himself had been too busy punching to hold on.

That was the biggest mistake The Kid ever made, for a split second of respite was all Carpentier required to whip over the fastest right-hand punch in the world. It came out of the smoky haze of the ring in a flash . . . a terrible blow on the point of Lewis's chin. No man living could have taken it and kept on his feet. The Kid toppled forward as though a bullet had pierced his brain. His corner protested, and the crowd began to boo.

Strictly speaking, Carpentier had not broken any rule, because the laws of boxing demand that a contestant must defend himself at all times, but it shook those of us who cherish real sportsmanship. "Peggy" Bettinson leaned over my shoulder and remarked: "Lewis was unlucky to-night. He would have won. He has already pricked the Carpentier bubble."

Before the contest Lewis had agreed to join Carpentier in a lunch to honour Jack Dempsey who had sat at the ringside. The Kid was furious with Carpentier's tactics, and angry with Dempsey who had loaned his name to an article on the fight which appeared in a morning paper. Ted was in such fighting mood that he told me before the lunch that he was going to tell Carpentier and Dempsey to their faces what he thought of them, and that if either wanted trouble they could have it on the spot. Knowing The Kid's fearlessness I hadn't the slightest doubt that in his present mood he was likely to swing a punch at both the heavy and light-heavyweight champions of the world. So I took him into a corner and told him that in the interest of himself and of British sport he would be making a terrible mistake if he started any trouble.

Finally, the Kid saw reason, and to his credit he swallowed his pride and warmly shook both Carpentier and Dempsey by the hand when they arrived. It was a fine gesture for a man who would have been happier starting up a free-for-all. Something happened to Lewis after that right-hander from Carpentier. He was never the same fighter again. His snap wilted, his fighting legs became anchored by lead, and his stamina ran out. He fought for three more years, but it was just the ghost of The Kid who dropped decisions to Augie Ratner, Roland Todd and lost his British welterweight title to a young up-and-coming Scot named Tommy Milligan.

In 1925 he had five fights and lost three of them, being disqualified. One of these bouts was a return with Milligan at the Albert Hall and The Kid, almost 30, hung his head as he left the ring to the hooting and hissing of the crowd after the

111

referee had ordered him to the dressing room for persistent holding.

I thought that night how cruel a fight crowd can be. Admittedly, a fading Lewis had ignored the official's warning and deserved the sentence, but if only that crowd had stopped to think of the good times Lewis had given them, and shown just a little mercy. If only they held back their boos and hissing and allowed him shame-faced to creep to his dressing room he would have been sufficiently punished by the chilly silence of a crowd that once had roared for him.

And so the curtain fell a little grimly on the career of Ted Lewis—the East End Kid who, in fifteen years' battling, earned a fortune exceeding £150,000 but had not kept a penny of it. A couple of years ago boxing came to his assistance, staging a large benefit tournamet.

It will be many years before Aldgate ever produces another Kid Lewis. Whitechapel did give us Judah Bergman, better known as Jack Kid Berg, a non-stop tear-away fighter who did more in the early thirties than any other British fighter to lift up our then desperately low boxing prestige in America.

Although he had fought at Premierland as "Young Yiddle," Berg made his name in America when he stormed his way to the top hammering out victories over Kid Chocolate, Tony Canzoneri, Mushy Callahan and Billy Petrolle. He was later beaten in world title bouts by Canzoneri, but he came home to win the lightweight title from another Jewish champion, Harry Mizler of St. Georges.

To-day Aldgate and Whitechapel haven't a Ted Kid Lewis or a Jack Kid Berg, but the race that once produced Daniel Mendoza is sure to provide boxing with another immortal who will punch his name on the fistic scroll of fame. I may not be around when this young Hebrew appears on the horizon. If not, I know I can leave him to the capable pen of Frank, who knows the fight game backwards. With that confidence I now hand you over to him to present to you tales of the more modern Kings of the Ring.

112

PART TWO

CHANGING HORSES IN MID-STREAM

BY

FRANK BUTLER

CHANGING HORSES IN MID-STREAM

IN TAKING OVER the reins in mid-stream from such an accomplished and respected boxing writer as my father, I realise I am tackling a precarious task—the toughest assignment any modern sports writer could possibly face. I'm prejudiced but sincere in my belief that there isn't a writer to-day who has twenty-five per cent of James Butler's knowledge of the fight game. He saw the bare-knuckle pugilists and went through the hardest possible apprenticeship, and for fifty-five years has concentrated on the ONE sport of boxing. To-day's qualifications for success as a critic of the toughest sport in the world seems to be a flare for sensational writing, a complete library of boxing books for reference, and the witnessing of half a dozen big fights. After this, one can apparently become overnight the greatest and most knowledgeable fight critic of all-time. It is a sad reflection that Fleet Street to-day has little time left for the expert and, because of this, accurate reporting of what really happens in a big fight is becoming less and less important.

Although I have been reporting boxing for the National Press now for more than 20 years, I haven't any hesitation in recording that James Butler has forgotten more about boxing and boxers than I shall ever learn. And I am proud to confess that anything I do know about the fight game has been taught me by my father.

My real interest in boxing began in a big way on September 16, 1923. That was the morning of my seventh birthday. As a special treat my father took me to Shoeburyness to watch the famed French light-heavyweight, Georges Carpentier, in training for his second fight with Joe Beckett.

It's strange, but it is often easier to remember more clearly the things that occurred thirty years ago than incidents of thirty months ago. I suppose it is because a greater impression is made on the mind of a child who has less to cram into his young brain than an adult.

Certainly, I can picture the Shoeburyness scene more than 30 years ago as though it were only yesterday. The amazing Monsieur François Descamps was there to meet us. So was Gus Wilson, who trained Carpentier, and Tom Berry, the old English heavyweight, who was acting as sparring partner to the Frenchman.

Gus Wilson and Carpentier made a great fuss of me, and on hearing it was my seventh birthday took me to the nearest sweet shop and purchased a 1 lb. box of King George V chocolates. Carpentier had reserved himself a warm and permanent corner in my young heart!

Shoeburyness is a pretty dead town on Sundays, and the likeable Frenchman seized the slightest chance of breaking the boredom of training. He took me to a street corner where the Salvation Army band had gathered. He placed one of the women's bonnets on my head and one of the men's peak caps on his own head and, borrowing the cymbals, joined in. Such was his charm and friendly smile that nobody seemed perturbed for he certainly showed no disrespect to the men and women in the blue and red uniform.

All this may seem far removed from boxing, but I am relating it because it was my early association with Georges Carpentier that caused me to make up my mind at the age of seven to become a boxing writer. Before I was ten I had made frequent visits to the old National Sporting Club in Covent Garden, to Premierland, the Blackfriars Ring and the Albert Hall while Harry Jacobs was still promoting, and to Olympia before C. B. Cochran finally turned his back on boxing.

Thanks to my father—I usually sat on the edge of two press seats, one used by my dad and the other by Charlie Rose or the late Freddie Dartnell—I was fortunate in being able to see some of the old-timers like Ted Kid Lewis, Ernie Rice, Harry Mason perform.

116

I never saw Jimmy Wilde in action, but I grew up knowing him and liking him soon after his retirement when he was becoming even more popular than when he was fighting. In fact, I grew up with the fight boys and soon became known as Jimmy Butler's boy. Promoters like Jeff Dickson, Sydney Hulls and Johnny Best were always kind to me, and long before I was 14 I was accepted as the friend of referees like Sam Russell, C. B. Thomas, the late Jack Smith, and of most managers, trainers and seconds.

At 16 I joined the *Daily Express* as a junior Editorial member of the Sports Department, and at 18 I was reporting football and boxing under my own name. I was given tremendous help and encouragement by Trevor Wignall, the first of the successful British sports columnists as we know them now. I did dressing room interviews for Trevor, and he was the first to give full credit for any good work I did—a gesture that meant so much to a young reporter anxious to make good. I became the boxing writer and columnist of the *Daily Express*, until in 1949 I was approached by the *News of the World* to take over the sports column of the paper with the largest circulation in the world.

Having given you these few details of how it all began I shall now endeavour to hold your interest with personal stories of some of the great modern Kings of the Ring.

CHAPTER I

SUGAR MELTS AT YANKEE'S INFERNO

It is 10 o'clock on the night of June 25, 1952. New York is sagging and melting under one of its heatwaves. As the temperature soars towards the nineties, the humidity is such that your shirt and trousers stick to your sweaty body like a wet swim suit. You don't mind the heat, but you feel sooner or later you'll stop breathing unless one puff of air finds its way across the Hudson. The breeze never comes. You manage to keep breathing, but you don't know how.

You agree New York City is no place for any guy in his right mind to hang around to-night. Yet there are millions of guys—and dolls—who aren't in their right minds. For there they are milling on Broadway . . . milling towards any air-conditioned buildings . . . movie-houses, hotels, bars and restaurants where it is wonderful to breathe freely again and to peel your shirt or blouse from your perspiring body like unwrapping a sticky toffee.

But where we are right now it is worse than Broadway. There is no air-conditioning. In fact, as we sit we are being toasted and grilled by a blaze of arc lights which rocket the temperature up to 104. Where are we—in Hades? It is an inferno anyway. The Yankee Stadium Inferno, and in this pressure cooker we sit and stew in the Press seats below 40 blazing, powerful, scorching television and ring lights as 31-year-old Sugar Ray Robinson, the kinky pompadoured king, who was never beaten as a welterweight, who now holds the world middleweight title, and who is about to try to bring off what only two other ring greats, Bob Fitzsimmons and Henry Armstrong, achieved—to lift a third world crown from light-heavyweight champion Joey Maxim.

118

We are literally melting at the ringside. Our jackets and neckties have been long since stripped off. Our American shirts are unbuttoned and pulled back so that we have little more covering us than the two fighters now in the ring. Fat men look revolting as grease drips from double chins. Embarrassed women, not so lucky as their menfolk when it comes to stripping, make futile attempts to wipe away mascara as it attempts to blend with their rouge. I look across at Peter Wilson, perspiring and thumping away at a typewriter. Lainson Wood, nearly 17 stone, looks as though he is in a Turkish Bath.

The green paint on the Press desks sticks to our trousers and to our copy paper. We keep buying canned beer, because our mouths are parched, our throats sore, and our tongues feel as rough as dry rope. I can recall only one man who doesn't look uncomfortable. He is General Douglas MacArthur, who is in a Working Press seat immediately behind me. The General, who is the subject of tremendous controversy, having been ordered home from the Far East by President Truman, is wearing a lightweight suit. He is lean and grey-looking but so cool and calm. There isn't a man near him who hasn't stripped off his jacket. I leaned over the back of my chair and asked: "General, who do you like—Robinson or Maxim?"

General MacArthur answers quietly, with a slight twinkle in his eye! "I don't follow fighting, but I should think Robinson."

It is unbearable at the ringside, but what is it going to be like inside the ropes when the Maxim-Robinson barbecue gets going?

Robinson has weighed in earlier in the day at 11st. 3½lbs., Maxim at 12st. 5lbs., but the fight which has been postponed for two days owing to rain is turning towards Robinson's favour. They reckon Maxim has had difficulty making the weight. He has trained down from nearly 14 stone, and the two days' postponement is supposed to be in Sugar's favour. If it goes more than 10 rounds Maxim will fade in this heat, say the wise boys.

The gong sounds, and Robinson bounds from his corner like

119

a young kangaroo. All his natural footwork, that enabled him to become an accomplished disciple of the famed Bojangles of Harlem, Bill Robinson, is at his command. Although some 16lbs., lighter, he is moving in, jabbing with a beautiful left. Now Maxim, whose real name is Guiseppe Berardinelli, is never brilliant. He is a strong son of Italian parents, and is described by U.S. fight fans as a plodder. There isn't any dynamite in his fighting make-up like there is in Sugar Ray. To-night Robinson makes Maxim appear a slow cart-horse thrown into the same paddock with a Kentucky Derby winner.

For round after round Robinson is the dancing master. He keeps . . . jab . . .jab . . . jabbing with that left all the time scoring points. He is light on his feet and is quickly out of trouble. But what a pace he is setting. Can Maxim last? That is what we begin saying. Nobody, after six rounds with Robinson five rounds ahead on points, thinks of asking: Will Sugar melt first? Maxim is dull to watch, but he is as strong as an ox, and when he gets inside he thumps left and right hooks at the sepia-skinned torso in front of him. Robinson doesn't like these blows, and who am I to blame him? Sugar holds on tightly to Maxim's arms and the tubby referee Ruby Goldstein, once a useful boxer, is working hard to separate the pair.

As we come into the seventh round it looks ten to one on Robinson. Maxim still has done little, and now the coloured fighter is not only jabbing with his left, but is crossing with right handers and left hooks to Maxim's iron jaw. Joey is shaken once or twice, but comes back plodding towards the black prince dancing before him.

Little do we realise this is the last desperate gamble of the great welter and middleweight king to win his third world crown. As Robinson returns to his corner at the end of this round he sags to his stool. His legs are going back on him. Maxim is too tough to be knocked out. Sugar has thrown in every big gun and has failed to halt this man who is too big and strong for him. If only he were four or five years younger he would then give this big cumbersome ox a boxing lesson.

Robinson keeps going like the great champ he is. But you can see his grip on the fight slipping. You can see Maxim getting stronger as Sugar Ray is beginning to melt like snow beneath the sun. Yet Maxim is still not doing enough to assure us he is going to win. He is 'way behind on points, and will he run out of rounds before he catches up? He can only win by a knockout. Just before the tenth round starts the effect of the dreadful heat is realised when Ruby Goldstein grabs a phial of smelling salts and warns New York State Athletic Commission officials he may not be able to carry on much longer. The heat is getting him; his head is swimming.

Sugar's head is swimming, too. His legs are like columns of lead. The spring has gone and he is flat-footed, but he is still trying to stay the distance . . . to hold on to his vast points lead. He slumps on his stool at the end of the tenth, but is in better shape than the referee who staggers across the ring like a drunken man, and is replaced by Ray Miller. The new referee brings a definite advantage to Maxim. Goldstein had wrestled with the boxers, and Joey's body attack in the clinches was restricted. Miller does not get between the boxers like Goldstein and Maxim is punching holes in Robinson's wasp-like body.

Maxim wins rounds 11 and 12. Sugar's eyes are wide and frightened . . . he is not afraid of Maxim, but he is afraid as he realises that for the first time in his golden career something is about to happen to him . . . something that for twelve years had always happened to the other guy. He is about to collapse. He no longer has control of himself.

The thirteenth round sees the end. Maxim realising certain defeat has turned into almost certain victory comes forward like a gigantic tank. He crashes into Robinson, now swinging rights to the head as well as left hooks to the body. Then Robinson attempts a desperate right . . . just like the desperate punch he swung when he was all but beaten in the second Turpin fight. Against Turpin the gamble came off— against Maxim it fails. He misses completely and, because his legs have gone, he falls flat on his face almost too weary to rise.

He drags himself to his feet, but wilts before Maxim's now ferocious body attack. Mechanically he back-pedals, but it is a matter of time now. When the gong sounds the end of the thirteenth, Sugar Ray is too dazed, too sick to know or to care what is happening. He staggers to a neutral corner "out on his feet." His seconds rush to assist him to his corner. George Gainford works furiously on him, frustrated by the knowledge that his fighter is still ahead on points and must win if, by some miracle, he can stand on his feet for the fourteenth and fifteenth rounds.

The gong sounds. The fourteenth round is on. Maxim rushes across the ring. The referee leaves his neutral corner, but Robinson is still slumped on his stool. He won't, or he can't continue. If he staggers to his feet he will soon be carried back to his corner. And so Sugar Ray Robinson, the finest welterweight and middleweight I have seen, fails to win his third world crown. But what a glorious failure!

Even Maxim supporters are silent. 50,000 fight fans stand as, amid funeral gloom, Sugar Ray is carried from the ring to his dressing room. It isn't just that another pugilist has gone to defeat. It is more than that. The crowd realise the great Robinson is passing over the fistic horizon, and they know fighters like him only come along once or perhaps twice in a generation. The fact that Robinson has picked up a nice little £65,000 for his efforts doesn't seem to count. The crowd mourn his defeat.

In the dressing room Maxim, cock-a-hoop, confesses he began to get worried round about the twelfth round. "I knew I was going to catch up with him" he tells me, "but I began to get anxious whether I would run out of rounds." On this one of New York's hottest nights, Maxim sweated off 7lbs. in 13 rounds of fighting. Robinson lost 5lbs. and, believe it or not, but I was 3lbs. lighter on the scales the morning after the night I shall never forget.

Having given unbiased praise of Robinson as one of the greatest fighters of the past thirty years, I must confess I am not one of Sugar Ray's admirers *OUTSIDE* the ring. I could never respect him as a man as I do Joe Louis.

Louis was not only a wonderful fighter, but a superb ambassador of the coloured race. But nothing can detract from the magnificence of Robinson inside the ropes. A fighting machine with the feather-steps of Bojangles, the snake-hips of a saronged beauty, and a punch as brutal as a trip-hammer.

I never knew Jack Johnson, but Robinson surely is the nearest approach to the former heavyweight champ in fistic ability plus the arrogance, pride, vanity and flashiness of the man who liked to be known as Lil' Arthur.

Robinson's great fistic hero as a kid was Joe Louis, yet he did not imitate the Brown Bomber's style inside or outside the ring. Louis was sultry, sleepy dynamite and flat-footed in action. He shuffled and stalked his opponents. When ready for the kill, he struck with the speed of a cobra. Robinson's opponents will describe him as a ball of fire, an energetic dancing master, unable to keep still for one moment from the time he left his dressing room until back on the rubbing table with yet another victim to be added to the long list in his remarkable record.

Louis was modest outside the ring. He spoke very little when not with intimate friends, unless, of course, he was giving one of those mass-interviews to the boxing writers.

Robinson is as loud as Louis is quiet, and often truculent and resentful in interviews. He has a bad habit of making statements which he so often denies later. At Pompton Lakes, when training for the second Turpin fight, I heard him violently accuse a respected New York boxing correspondent, Jim Burchard, of misquoting him the previous day. Burchard was as angry as Robinson at the accusation, and in no uncertain terms put the flashy champion in his place. Hence this gag among some of the U.S. boxing writers:

"What statement is Robinson gonna deny to-day?"

I do not criticise Robinson for his affection of the loud things of life. Everybody is entitled to his own taste, and good luck to him if he can afford to own at one go 50 suits, 25 pairs of shoes, dozens of sports jackets and silk shirts all monogrammed "Sugar." Good luck to him also for being in the financially-happy position to have purchased a fuschia-coloured Cadillac convertible (also well-monogrammed "Sugar" in front and along the panels of the doors) all because he wanted a car to match his favourite tie!

To invade Europe he collected the loudest circus that any pugilist has attempted. But why not? That was his business.

Like Johnson before him, Robinson stopped the traffic in Paris where a coloured man of fame is always fêted. On the Champs-Élysées beautiful white women gathered outside the swank Claridge's Hotel and goggled at the handsome Brown Tornado, surrounded by such Runyonlike characters as Bang Bang Womber (chief sparring partner), George Gainford (Falstaffian manager), Shelton Oliver (permanent golf professional hired to keep Sugar's swing smooth), Roger Simon (personal barber who is well paid to give Sugar's hair a parting and iron out the natural kinks . . . a losing battle because Robinson's hair resorts to its natural fuzziness after a few minutes inside the ropes), Jimmy Karoubi (a 36-inch dwarf added to the circus in Paris as a publicity stunt), June Clark (his secretary—a male in spite of the fancy name), Pee Wee Beale (trainer), Honey Brewer (second trainer and brother-in-law), to say nothing of two attractive women, Edna Mae (his wife, a former show girl) and Evelyn (his sister).

London was less adoring than Paris, but, nevertheless, amazed when this colourful party descended with nearly 100 suitcases and "Flamingo"—pet name for the Cadillac—especially driven from Dover to London by a French chauffeur.

The party cost Robinson an average of £50 a day to keep in Paris and London. And one-way fares amounted to more than £2,000.

It was all good ballyhoo and good business, because Sugar Ray's income is such that the tax man is quick to grab and slow in mercy unless Robinson can produce some pretty hefty expense chits. He succeeded in achieving this on his fantastic European tour.

But behind all this publicity and flashiness, Robinson at least wasn't a phony publicity seeker. I rate him, in fact, as the finest welterweight I ever saw . . . and the top middleweight, although I emphasise that Sugar's best fighting days were seen when he was knocking over opponents of 10st. 7lbs. And for all his truculence and unreliable statements, there is one thing that must be said in favour of Robinson . . . he never forgot the goodness of his mother towards him when he was a poor child in Detroit and later in New York. When he became champion he bought her a nice house, and publicly announced: "I owe everything I am to-day to Mama."

Robinson was born Walker Smith Junior in Detroit's Paradise Valley—the Harlem of New York—on May 3, 1920. His old man walked out on Sugar's mother and three kids and has not been heard of since. The boy was seven at the time, and his two sisters a few years older. Mrs. Walker Smith went to work as a seamstress to keep her children from hunger and nakedness.

Young Walker Smith began picking up a few dimes washing windows, shoe-shining and delivering newspapers. And sometimes he earned extra dimes tap-dancing on the sidewalks. Such was his natural ability with his feet that he could always attract a crowd of passers-by to admire his lightness of foot.

He had three boyhood heroes . . . Ty Cobb, the baseball star, Joe Louis, who was only a few years older than himself, and Bill Robinson, the dancer. It was a toss-up whether he became a dancer or a fighter, but the fact that he took the name Robinson was not in honour of the famed dancer. It just happened that one night at Waterbury, Connecticut, Walker Smith was watching a tournament. One of the fighters didn't turn up and George Gainford, who was already looking after the interests of Walker Smith, was asked if he could find a deputy. Gainford and young Smith exchanged one glance only and it was settled. The snag was that Walker Smith wasn't licensed and didn't possess the necessary A.A.U. card. Gainford got round this by borrowing a licence from a coloured boy named Ray Robinson, who was attending the tournament but was not competing.

Walker Smith won this bout in convincing fashion, and began to get plenty of offers to box in many of the amateur bootleg clubs where trophies were presented in public and later exchanged for cash in the back room.

He stuck to his new name. The real Ray Robinson never followed the pathway to fame as a fighter, and went into oblivion after being called into Uncle Sam's Army during the war. Another title was added to Walker Smith's fighting nom-de-guerre when a boxing writer turned to George Gainford and remarked with admiration: "Gee, George, you've sure got a sweet fighter there . . . yes, as sweet as Sugar." To-day Walker Smith is internationally known as Sugar Ray Robinson.

There wasn't any stopping the Sugar Boy now. He blitzed his way through the amateurs, and was never defeated in 125 bouts. Of 89 registered amateur contests, Robinson won 68 by a knockout. In 1939 he won the Golden Gloves featherweight crown, and in 1940 collected the lightweight title.

Mike Jacobs, who had earlier signed Joe Louis up for sole rights, was now casting ambitious eyes towards Robinson. He wanted to be sure to get in first with a monopoly contract. So Sugar Ray said farewell to the amateurs in October 1940 when he made his pro' début in New York, knocking out one Joe Echeverria in 2 rounds. That same night another great coloured boxer, Henry Armstrong, who had held three world titles, reached near the end of the trail when on the same bill he lost his welterweight title to hard-punching Fritzie Zivic. After winning his own bout, the 20-year-old Sugar sat sadly watching the great Armstrong chopped about by Zivic. He vowed that he would never end up like that but would retire one day an undefeated world champion.

Gainford and Robinson needed money and plenty of it

quickly. So they did a deal with a wealthy beer magnate, Kurt Horrman. It was agreed Horrman should become sole manager, Gainford carrying on as head-trainer. Horrman agreed to pay a weekly sum of money to Robinson to enable him to live comfortably and to look after his mother. The beer magnate also agreed to pay the cost of Robinson's divorce from his first wife whom he had married when he was sixteen . . . a marriage which had lasted only a few months but had produced a baby son.

Horrman soon found he had a handful in the flashy, cocky, arrogant kid from Detroit. At twenty-one—and with less than twelve months' professional boxing behind him—Robinson had beaten top men like Sammy Angott, world lightweight champion, Fritzie Zivic, who had lost the world welterweight title a few months earlier, Marty Servo and Maxie Shapiro.

Ray was already hitting the high-spots, buying himself tuxedoes, flashy cars, and was convinced he could lick the world without even training. He had won more than 30 consecutive pro fights mostly by knockout when Horrman had enough of him. They had words and Robinson and Gainford bought the contract for £2,500, Gainford taking over . . . although I have always understood that Ray insisted Gainford had to accept a smaller percentage than most American fight managers who insist on a fifty-fifty split of all purses.

Robinson is, and always has been, the boss in his training camp. He cleverly allows Gainford to do the talking, but Robinson decides what fights he will take and uses his fat manager as the stooge whenever he wishes to deny earlier statements that are not any longer convenient to his plans.

His love of dancing has never waned. He is mad about movies, playing cards, gambling, theatres and golf. It was Joe Louis who really started Robinson as a golfer. When the Brown Bomber took up the game, dozens of Negro fighters like Robinson, Ike Williams followed suit. Louis was such a hero among them all, that whatever he did was sure to be copied by hundreds of adoring young Negroes.

127

Like Louis, Robinson invested a fortune in real estate. He was better advised than the old heavyweight champion, and to help himself against heavy taxation formed a corporation with a block in Harlem which he has named Ray Robinson Enterprises Incorporated. This block consists of a couple of dozen apartments, the Golden Gloves Barber's Shop, Sugar Ray's Quality Cleaners and Dyers, Sugar Ray's Bar and Restaurant and Edna Mae Lingerie. The total business is reckoned to be worth a quarter of a million pounds. On top of this, this fistic cutie runs a loan business.

Robinson lost his popularity in America for a time after being medically discharged from the Army shortly before he was due to go overseas. Since the end of the war he has strived to regain popularity, and has succeeded in most places. He can thank much of this to Walter Winchell who has "plugged" Robinson in his column telling all the things the coloured boxer has done for the Damon Runyon Cancer Fund.

Robinson took himself too seriously at a Press luncheon party at Windsor when he was training for the first Turpin fight. He told us he hadn't really come to England to fight but firstly to hand a cheque from the Runyon fund to a cancer fund in this country. The fact that Robinson was collecting £28,000 for fighting Turpin didn't apparently have anything to do with his visit!

But let us not dwell further on Robinson the man. Let us praise him as a superb fighting machine who, at the time of writing, has only dropped three decisions in 266 amateur and professional fights.

He was undefeated as a light and welterweight. Only two middleweights, Jake LaMotta and Randy Turpin, ever defeated him. Robinson dropped a points decision to LaMotta in one of his bouts when he wasn't bothering about training, but he more than squared that defeat with five victories over LaMotta. He lost his title to Turpin in London, which was the biggest boxing turn-up of 1951. The British champion boxed like an angel that night, although, in fairness to Sugar

FRANK BUTLER

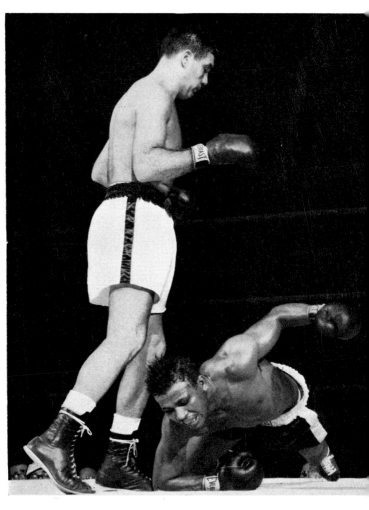

Sugar Ray's last fight. Sugar Ray Robinson falls flat after missing with a right
in his world light-heavyweight bid against Joey Maxim. The fight took
place in New York's Yankee Stadium on June 19, 1952. Ringside temperature was 104°. Robinson finally collapsed and failed to come up for the
14th round. The referee had collapsed earlier.

Ray, Paris isn't the ideal training ground for a world title fight.

Robinson avenged this defeat knocking out Turpin in the return fight in New York 64 days later. He proved himself a real champion by producing a Sunday punch just at a time when he looked certain of defeat.

His only other defeat was at the hands of the light-heavyweight champion of the world, Joey Maxim, and of that fight I have already told you plenty.

The finest thing I can say about Robinson's fistic ability is that when he came on his two barn-storming trips to Europe, he had already seen his best fighting days. In spite of this, he was still a sensation, first in Paris where I saw him dispose of Jean Stock in two rounds in 1950 while the members of his circus hopped and sprang around the ring like black frogs in blue sweaters. He then bowled over Luc Van Dam in Brussels, Robert Villemain in Paris, Hans Stretz in Frankfurt and Jean Walzack in Geneva. These four fights brought him £16,000. He had trouble in Berlin in 1951 when 30,000 Germans protested he had hit Gerhard Hecht in the kidneys. He was disqualified in the second round amid uproar. So angry were the fight fans that Robinson had to take up an undignified hiding place beneath the ring as bottles, chairs and anything handy were thrown at him. Police escorted him to his dressing room.

Next day the West Berlin Boxing Commission altered the referee's decision and declared the fight to be "no contest," and his £5,000 purse was paid him in full. He then massacred the Belgian champion Cyril Delannoit at Turin in July, 1951 in a matter of minutes, and came on to London wrongly believing he would have a nicely paid picnic against Randy Turpin at Earl's Court.

In a later chapter I will tell you why Robinson was lucky to regain his middleweight title from Turpin in New York. Jack Solomons tried everything to get Sugar in a third time with the British champion at White City a week before the Coronation of Queen Elizabeth II. But I am convinced that Robinson, realising how close he had come to defeat again in the second Turpin fight, never intended going in the ring a third time with the British champion, because Robinson knew he had left his best fighting days behind him.

The fact that he ducked Turpin and chose retirement rather than defeat doesn't alter the fact that Sugar Ray Robinson, alias Walker Smith, in his prime was one of the most accomplished welter and middleweights the world has known.

CHAPTER II

THE TONYPANDY KID

ONE SUNDAY MORNING in April, 1950, Tommy Farr 'phoned me from Brighton. "Get yourself down here for lunch, m'dear," sang the man who, nearly thirteen years earlier, had come within a point or fraction of a point of lifting the world heavyweight title from Joe Louis, and then added: "I want your advice in confidence." Over the telephone Tommy always addresses me as "m'dear" and as one of his oldest friends among the boxing writers, I readily accepted this invitation to me as a pal rather than as a reporter.

At Hove I found Tommy to all outward appearances relaxed and without a care in the world. He was the perfect host. We wined and dined like millionaires. Then, when the coffee arrived, he shot at me almost aggressively as though anticipating opposition: "I'm making a come-back, Frank. I know I can lick the present bunch of heavyweights and, what's more, I can take care of Pat Comiskey, Lee Savold and Joe Baksi." He paused and added: "This by the way, m'boy, is not for publication. I'm talking to you now under the old pal's act."

I didn't reply immediately. I knew all was not well with Tommy financially. He had retired rich in 1940 . . . rich at least for a fighter in those days before inflated purses and King Solomons had arrived. He had become such a successful businessman, running a pub known as Tommy Farr's Corner. Later he took over a restaurant which he called Tommy Farr's Pantry. He was in a highly successful bookmaking business—South Coast Commissions—and he had speculated with valuable properties. I believe also he had been a lucky gambler on horses, dogs and the Stock Exchange, but his luck had changed and all was not well.

I knew things must have been pretty bad for Tommy to entertain the idea of returning to a tough sport to which he had once kissed good-bye with a nice swag in his pocket.

For ten years he had lived softly. By softly, I mean out of training, attending the occasional cocktail party and smoking reasonably heavy. Also he was 36 years of age—ancient as boxers go. Ten years out of the rings trips most fighters off their timing, reflexes and toughness.

Farr must have read my mind. "Well?" he inquired, "You don't think I can fight any more?" Farr never once mentioned his financial worries. I admired him for it.

"If you HAVE to fight, I suppose you must," I stammered rather feebly, "but you know, Tommy, they just never come back."

"Listen, Frank Butler," snorted Farr, "do you mean to say you don't think I can lick the likes of Jack Gardner, Johnny Williams and the rest. As for Savold and Baksi—they're just made for me."

"They wouldn't have placed a glove on the OLD Tommy Farr," I persisted, "but you can collect plenty of rust in ten years."

I was recalling the granite-like Farr who had walked into Max Baer, Walter Neusel and Joe Louis. A Welsh miner who had made the Yankees swallow their jibes about British horizontal heavyweight champions, for Farr had never been knocked out although he had fought Louis and had five fights with ex-world champions.

I was also thinking of his attractive wife Carole, better known as Monty—she was Miss Montgomery before marriage—and his three lovely kids Rosalind—she's known as Jo—Tommy—they call him Junior—and Cary, the image of his Old Man.

My final words of advice were: "Think it over again, Tommy. You know your own business but I hope you find another way of solving your problems." Yet I knew Tommy had made up his mind. It was two months later in Rio where I was reporting the World Soccer Cup that I read that Tommy Farr had officially announced his come-back.

I am sorry Tommy Farr had to fight again because any man who had risen out of the depths of squalor and poverty of the Welsh pits and who had battled so hard without credit before finally succeeding should not have to be called upon for a second helping of punishment. I am sorry he had to come back and walk into a sucker punch from Frank Bell, the schoolmaster from Barnoldswick, Yorkshire, and that the records now tell us that for the first time in his life Tommy Farr was knocked out in 2 rounds at Porth by a fighter who could not have placed a real punch on him ten years earlier.

But Farr's return not only helped Tommy out of any financial difficulties, but made us realise how much better the Tonypandy Kid was than we gave him credit for, and how far back boxing had gone since before the war. In his come-back he showed all the moves of the master. He made the best of them look silly. If he could have recaptured his youth he would have trotted home an easy winner over the Gardners, the Williams, the Baksis and the rest.

I confess I did not believe Farr could stand up for 10 rounds against moderate but youthful opposition. Yet he more than held his own until he retired after defeat by Don Cockell.

In 1926 at the age of 12 he began fighting for fame and fortune. In 1950 he began spilling more blood for his wife and three children. What finer motive could any man have?

Not everybody likes Farr. He has a long memory, is a good friend, but a tough enemy. He is realistic and down to earth—forthright if he doesn't like you.

One day he met Jack Petersen, who said with a smile: "You don't like me, do you?"

"No," replied Farr bluntly, and when pressed for the reason, he added: "When you had the title you would never give me a fight, and I don't like anybody who stops me earning my bread and butter!"

133

Had it not been for his enforced come-back, Tommy Farr would have come nearer than any other British fighter towards achieving some of the success of Gene Tunney. But the fates were not so kind to the Tonypandy Kid as they were to Tunney, and so Farr goes down as the British Gene Tunney who wasn't quite . . .

Like Tunney, Farr was brought up in poverty and, like the New York Irishman, Tommy's talents were recognised only grudgingly after years of striving. Tunney was considered a dull performer until near the end of his career when he whipped Dempsey twice, and in his last bout beat Tom Heeney in a world championship battle which brought him more criticism than praise from the boxing writers.

Farr spent years trying to get a title fight with Jack Petersen but couldn't get recognition from the Boxing Board of Control or the big promoters. They didn't consider the miner from Tonypandy box-office. Even though he received decisions over two ex-world light-heavyweight champions, Tommy Loughran and Bob Olin, London fight fans did not take to him. And because he was unwanted the Welshman, who had fought against hunger, developed a pretty large chip on his shoulder, learned to hate and became suspicious of everybody. He might just as well have strived to break the sound barrier as win over the hearts of London fight fans. He was then just a heavyweight without a big punch. A spoiler who tied up the other fellow, but didn't give the customers many thrills. And a heavyweight without a punch is as pleasing to the fight public as an ugly woman is to a man.

The Welshman's first fight in London was the most disastrous début that I have seen any great fighter make. It took place at the old Crystal Palace in 1933 a few months before I joined the *Daily Express*. Sydney Hulls had originally matched one of Phil Scott's white hopes, Eddie Steele of Norwood, with Randy Jones, the Welsh cruiserweight champion. Jones injured himself a few days before the fight so Hulls was advised to take as a substitute an 18-year-old miner from Tonypandy named Farr who had a month earlier beaten Jones. Every boxing writer who mattered was in Manchester that night for a championship fight, but I used my father's press ticket at the Palace.

Steele versus young Farr proved a terrible fight. There was holding and slapping, and little action. So much so that after 6 rounds the crowd set up the slow hand-clap and openly jeered. But suddenly in the 7th round Steele landed a moderate punch on Farr's throat. To my amazement the Welsh boy stopped boxing, vaulted the ropes and ran down the gangway to his dressing room with Steele, the referee, and his seconds looking after him in amazement. I have never seen any fighter, amateur or pro., do this. Farr disappeared into the Welsh hills for nearly 12 months, being undefeated in 15 bouts which included the winning of the Welsh light-heavyweight title from Randy Jones. He returned to London in February, 1934, to drop a decision to Eddie Phillips. Farr just could not gate-crash the big-time and he resented the opposition to him. He nursed what he considered to be a grave injustice until the most important battle the Welshman was engaged in was The World versus Tommy Farr. Even when eventually in 1937 he became British and Empire heavyweight champion, outpointing Ben Foord at Harringay in one of the dullest heavyweight championships I ever saw, he had still not melted the ice, London fight fans had built to keep him out of their hearts. The boxing writers were sarcastic; the crowds were cold. But nobody outside perhaps of Jobey Churchill, Tommy's old one-legged saddler friend from Tonypandy who gave Farr a wonderful philosophy and an education that could not have been equalled at Public School or University, knew the granite from which Farr had been moulded. Although his heart nursed hatred, it was also made of a substance more durable than the earth of Tonypandy beneath which he had once sweated. Few folk had ever approached close enough to gaze into the steel that flashed from clear blue eyes. They had never bothered to find out that beneath the rugged muscle and bone of the miner was a spirit more obstinate than any mule.

It was Farr's sincere belief that the world was against him that eventually made him into a successful fighter because, whether Tommy likes it or not, he was not a great fighter in my book until the night he so completely outboxed and outfought Maxie Baer at Harringay to upset the ridiculous odds of 10 to 1 against him. He made the boxing experts slip past him, their faces pink with embarrassment. The fickle boxing public forgot their deep-freeze attitude towards him. They switched on the heat, and following the immediate thaw their hearts glowed for Tommy Bach. That night at Harringay Englishmen, Irishmen, Scots and Jews stood on their feet and, without knowing the words, hummed in tune while the loyal contingent from Tonypandy moved our hearts with the talent of a professional choir but with more fervour as they nearly took the lid off Harringay with "Land of My Fathers."

Baer, the ex-world heavyweight champion, the fighter who possessed the hardest right hand punch of any fighter in the past twenty-five years including Louis, Schmeling and Marciano sat in his corner bemused, thumbing the blood as it poured down from a cut above his left eye. He was all at sea, thinking out loud: "These Limeys have taken me for a ride. They told me this Farr was a hunk of cheese who didn't know how to fight!"

Most Englishmen believed that Farr couldn't fight, and it was legalised slaughter to put him in the ring with Baer. Even the late Sydney Hulls, one of our great promoters, who brought Baer to England thought Farr was in for a hiding. But Hulls had gone to America earlier to bring Maxie to England to fight Jack Petersen. In the meantime, however, Jack unexpectedly lost his heavyweight title to Ben Foord in 3 rounds at Leicester. He later came out of a semi-retirement to take a third beating from Walter Neusel, the blond German who had also beaten Foord.

Hulls, therefore, had Baer on his hands committed by contract. He suggested a fight with Neusel, but the Boxing Board would not permit Hulls to match two foreigners so it had

136

to be Tommy. No wonder, therefore, that the Welshman was cynical when at the end he listened to the cheers of "Good old Tommy" from the fight mob at the ringside. He had a truculent grin on his face. Knowing him as I do I am sure he was getting a great kick at the faces of astounded boxing writers who were having a tough task in phoning their stories and explaining away that the Welsh boy had not been murdered by Baer. That, in actual fact, the man they had said couldn't fight was now contender for the World heavyweight championship. In one fight he had thumbed his nose at all his knockers. With 36 minutes of actual boxing he had achieved what he had failed to accomplish in six years of striving. Now the boot was on the other foot. Now he was the piper who would call the tune. If anybody else wanted to suggest any music, by gosh they were going to have to pay dearly for it!

A new Tommy Farr was born that night. He remained truculent, but his bitterness began to thaw and he mellowed quickly. All the natural wit, the philosophy he had learned from Jobey Churchill, a hidden charm and a spanking good sense of humour which had been bottled inside poured from him, and he was to become one of our most popular fighters.

Never had a British heavyweight handled a top American so easily as Farr toyed with Baer. The Welshman was cock-a-hoop, Sydney Hulls was on top of the world, and so were British fight fans.

Walter Neusel, slayer of British heavyweights, was next lined up at Harringay on June 15, 1937, and I can see Tommy smartly moving in and out for two rounds against the ponderous German who looked a novice. I have never seen a fighter so confident of himself as Farr that night, and when he advanced with a left and a right cross to Neusel's chin in the third round you could sense the end coming. Neusel, who already wore a knee support, collapsed, made a sort of attempt to rise, but quit cold on one knee.

It was a fiasco, but there wasn't any booing. 10,000 British fans delighted at the avenging of the defeats of Petersen, Foord and the rest, stood and cheered and sang.

Von Ribbentrop, then German Ambassador to Britain, left the ringside angry and embarrassed. The delighted Sydney Hulls now made a match between Max Schmeling and Farr to take place at White City, London, for which Farr would receive £7,500 and Schmeling £15,000. It was all agreed, but in the meantime Mike Jacobs, short of opponents for Joe Louis, who had won the world title from Jim Braddock exactly one week after Farr had beaten Neusel, made an attractive offer for Farr to fight Louis for the title in New York in August.

Although a contract had been signed for Hulls, Farr, tempted by the offer plus the fact that Schmeling might step in and fight Louis if he himself declined the offer, took the Louis engagement. And what a show the tough kid from Tonypandy put on. He wasn't given a chance by American or English fans, but he walked into Louis from the first gong as though the Brown Bomber was just a Bum. Had Farr not cut his eye in training a few days before the fight, he would have stood an even better chance of beating Louis that night.

Farr started under handicap when they called him to the ringside twenty minutes before the fight was due to begin. He sat watching the preliminary bout—a test even for a man of iron nerves. Yet when the first bell sounded, Tommy walked into Louis as though he were some sparring partner and jabbed a honey of a left into the champion's face. Tommy lured Louis to him, belted him about the body, and raised a lump under Joe's right eye.

Louis, puzzled by the Welshman's crouch and clever defence, took time to settle down, but soon he began to hand out terrific punishment opening up the cut beneath Tommy's right eye. But Farr did a job of work for British boxing that night.

The harder Louis smashed him with right crosses, the more determined the Welsh boy became as he kept boring in always attacking. The seventh was the most punishing and most exciting of the fight. Onlookers thought the Brown Bomber

138

was going to win by a knockout, but they didn't know the stuff Tommy Bach was made of. Three murderous left hooks had him spinning. A right hook brought more blood from the cut eye which dripped on to his chest. No previous opponent of Louis like Baer, Carnera, Braddock, Sharkey, Uzcudun, King Levinsky had been able to withstand this sort of punishment, but Farr, spitting blood from his mouth and thumbing it from his eyes, kept going in.

This was his crisis round and the crowd, pro-Louis at the start, were now on the side of the courageous Welshman. Joe was told to go out and finish the bout in the eighth round but his advisers underestimated Farr. The Tonypandy Kid was again carrying the battle to the world champion and jabbed Louis round the ring. Even when Joe smashed open his cuts again, Tommy grinned through the red mask and went on to win the round. He also won the ninth. Had Tommy Farr possessed a big punch in his right hand he must have won the world title now but, alas, Tommy was never a puncher although he jabbed, hurt and cut up his opponent with his left.

Louis was in most definite danger of losing his crown although, great champion that he was, he rallied to win several of the closing rounds and to take Arthur Donovan's decision, but it was mighty close. So close in fact that a large section of the crowd hooted the decision, although the two judges and referee scored decisively in favour of Louis. But Tommy Farr had never been more glorious.

Farr was in trouble with the Board of Control and Hulls when he returned to England. But he didn't care. He had thrown his lot entirely with Mike Jacobs who had promised him a return bout with Louis. Shrewd as Tommy was, I shall always consider he made his biggest mistake in not taking his next fight in Britain. He should have remained in England for one or two fights. In spite of their differences over the Schmeling business, Syd Hulls would have been delighted to have brought Max Baer back again or some other heavyweight, but Tommy was headstrong and instead of playing hard to catch went hurrying back at Mike's first call to take on James J. Braddock, the ex-champion, who had retired after losing his title to Louis. Farr's showing against the Negro world champion had been good enough to warrant a return title fight without any preliminaries, but Mike talked him into the Braddock match which proved to be disastrous and must have cost Tommy at least £50,000.

It was considered a good thing for the Welsh fighter but Braddock, a cute old-timer, tied the Welsh boy up sufficiently to win the sentiments of the crowd who began cheering home the underdog. Many experts thought Farr had done sufficient to win. Tommy was sure he had walked it, but the people who mattered—the judges—awarded the decision to Braddock, who promptly retired again on a winning note.

The bottom dropped out of Tommy's world when he lost the decision. He could not get a Louis match now. I still think he should have come home to defend his British title against Len Harvey or Eddie Phillips or to have a return with Baer in London. But on Jacobs' advice he fought Max Baer a return fight in New York and this time Maxie gave Farr a good beating, although the Welshman gave yet another display of great courage.

Poor Tommy! He had started in America at the top and worked his way down. After the defeat by Baer, Mike still gave him fights. But he lost first to Lou Nova and then to the moderate Red Burman, a protégé of Jack Dempsey. Five U.S. fights and all of them lost! All he had left to boast of was that he had finished on his feet every time.

The Burman defeat in January 1939, was Farr's American swan-song. He came home no longer British champion because he had ignored the earlier demands of the Board to return to defend his title, and Len Harvey had beaten Eddie Phillips for the championship which had been declared vacant. Farr was, in fact, suspended, not having paid the £750 the Boxing Board of Control had ordered him to pay Hulls for breach of contract over the Schmeling fight. Farr took the matter to the Stewards of Appeal but lost. Before he could fight in London he had **first** to pay the money. He did this in March, 1939, and was reinstated. The difference with Hulls was now patched up, and Red Burman was brought to England for a return fight at Harringay in April. Farr won, but it was disappointing and Tommy seemed to be in trouble several times when Burman threw a left hook.

After this Tommy was matched with Larry Gains at Cardiff in May—another disappointing fight with Gains retiring with a damaged hand after five rounds. Sydney Hulls had planned to bring Farr's American conquerors one by one to London . . . Nova, Baer, Braddock (if he could be persuaded) and then perhaps Louis. But war came in September. Tommy had only two minor bouts before retiring. He beat Manuel Abrew in three rounds in Dublin in November, 1939, and Zachy Nicholas at Barnstaple in August, 1940. He joined the R.A.F., but was medically discharged.

Tommy had done well for himself financially and had married an attractive wife. He had a business brain and everything went right for him. Everything he touched seemed to turn into gold.

In retirement he became a mellowed and popular character compared to the suspicious, belligerent fellow who at one time had thought the world was against him. He became a perfect host, a brilliant conversationalist, and good company to be around with.

I was sorry to see him come-back, but it was a tribute to his courage, stamina and skill that he did so well, often giving a boxing lesson to men fifteen years younger.

Time finally caught up with the Tonypandy Kid at Nottingham when he fought Don Cockell to find a challenger for Johnny Williams's title. Against Cockell, Tommy had come to the end of the road. His skill was still there, but his ammunition was wet. Cockell, a much better boxer than most folk credit him, outjabbed the man who had been boxing in booths as a kid before he himself was even born.

Farr's left eye was cut, and blood began to flow, but Tommy,

141

as always, refused to quit. Finally, the referee stopped a one-sided bout after seven rounds. Tommy was annoyed. He was not unduly distressed, and he wanted to go down fighting. But the referee acted wisely. Tommy didn't have a chance against his youthful opponent who went on to win the heavyweight title from Johnny Williams.

Yet the old warrior from Tonypandy stole the show at the finish. He grabbed the mike and sang from the heart the Welsh National Anthem. From the back of the Nottingham Ice Rink which holds but 6,000 fans, it seemed as though there was a choir of 10,000 Welshmen.

I was not the only hardened ringsider who felt a lump come into his throat that night. I looked up at the marked face of a great warrior who had been born at least fifteen years too soon. Had he arrived on the scene at the time of Woodcock, Gardner, Williams and Cockell, Tommy Farr may have become the first British heavyweight to win the world title since old Ruby Bob Fitzsimmons.

To-day we welcome him as the boxing columnist of the *Sunday Pictorial.* He is still punching away for the good of boxing.

CHAPTER III

"WHO D'YA LIKE—DEMPSEY OR LOUIS?"

"DEMPSEY WOULD HAVE massacred Louis . . . massacred him with one hand tied behind his back and one leg strapped to the ring post. To me there ain't no comparison between Dempsey and Louis. One was a killer who went in and mauled all opposition. Louis was a good fighter among a bunch of bums. I'd give Louis four rounds—and that's generous—against Dempsey at his best."

It was old "Doc" Kearns talking . . . Kearns, the man who had once steered Dempsey along a golden trail to the heavyweight championship of the world which included five separate million-dollar gates and earned Dempsey £1,500,000. The Doc had mellowed with the years. The fire had gone out of his conversation and he sipped only orange juice, because he had sworn off alcohol ever since he nearly went to jail for a long stretch over a deal which he became entangled with when drunk.

There were a dozen of us sitting in Dempsey's restaurant on Broadway this June night in 1951, whiling away a couple of hours prior to the big fight in Madison Square Garden between Joe Louis, making one more bid to get another crack at the world title, and Lee Savold.

At our table was Bill Daly, manager of Savold, Ray Arcel, prince of trainers, Charlie Johnston, manager of Archie Moore and Sandy Saddler, and a bunch of the fight mob, who never tire of talking fights and fighters from the time they get up after the streets are well aired until the time they go to bed not many hours before the ordinary office worker is about to rise.

Dempsey himself was in town for the fight, and had stopped at our table for a quick "How'ya fellows." As the old champ left, one of the mob, for want of something better to say, started the old controversy: "I wonder what would have happened had that guy met Louis when they were both in their prime."

Kearns took over from there. The old Doc and Dempsey had been bad friends for a number of years over a little thing called money but had patched up their quarrel recently, and were now on nodding terms. "Jack and I had our differences," added Kearns, "but what a fighter he was . . . the greatest of all-time. As for Louis, tell me who did the guy ever beat? Go on, tell me."

I was sitting back quietly sipping a beer, because I had no ammunition to fire yet. Kearns was a man of nearly seventy. He had lived a full life, and had steered Dempsey from the bad days when both had been near starving to the richest prize in the world of sport.

"Perhaps the Doc is prejudiced," I thought to myself, "or perhaps, like so many old-timers, he is living in the past." As we get older it seems we link our finest and happy memories with the days gone by. Haven't you heard your parents or grandparents declare the old days were the best and happiest? It's the same with old-timers in boxing. The champs they knew were the best. Maybe they were, because those who have lived longer hold the advantage of having seen the past as well as the present.

And as I get older the champions I watched as a young man will probably grow in prestige and greatness rather than fade.

But at least Doc Kearns had left himself open. He had said something that allowed a younger man to step in, and I took my chance like an eager young fighter seeing the old champ drop his guard for a split second.

"Who did Louis beat, Doc?" I inquired. "Guys like Carnera, Sharkey, Schmeling, Baer, Braddock, Farr, Galento, Nova, Conn, Mauriello and Jersey Joe Walcott . . . to name a few."

"Bums!" hissed back Kearns, "Every one of them bums. Dempsey would have paralysed them all."

"Well, Joe Louis didn't exactly treat them like dolls, did he Doc?" I replied, "Apart from Farr, he knocked them all out, and a guy can do no more than flatten the best opposition of his day. When he lost to Ezzard Charles and got knocked out by Marciano he was through as a great fighter."

"Sure thing," grinned old Kearns, "Louis was a good fighter. He was too good for the bums he had to fight, but there wasn't a Dempsey around which was lucky for Louis."

"Now," I thought, "is the time to play my trump card," and I shot it more at the company than at Kearns.

"Well, if it comes down to hard facts, tell me—who did Dempsey beat?" The boys were laughing as the old Doc snapped back. "Who did Jack beat? I'll tell you. He massacred a giant named Jess Willard, he k.o'd Billy Miske, Bill Brennan, Carpentier. He whipped Tommy Gibbons and knocked out another giant called Firpo . . . all good fighters."

"But weren't they also bums?" I asked, encouraged by the twinkle in the eyes of Daly, Arcel and the rest. "Would Miske or Brennan or Carpentier, who was only a light-heavyweight anyway, and Willard and Firpo have licked Louis? And didn't the first guy who could really box and take a punch, Gene Tunney, lick him?"

"Say, you've got something there, Frank," said Bill Daly, "Dempsey was a great fighter, but he was as outstanding in his generation as Louis has been in his. Some of these Dempsey victims were bums, and a smart fellow like Tunney came up and licked him. We were all shocked by this result in 1926, mainly because Dempsey had never been extended before apart from Firpo who dropped him."

Kearns was just about to tell me what Miske or Brennan or Firpo would have done to Louis when Ray Arcel broke up the little party: "Hi, fellows, it's getting late. We'll give our verdict after the fight."

And so we filed out of Dempsey's, expressing our different views as we walked the couple of blocks over to the Garden to watch a Louis who at 37 was almost over the hill.

I wasn't thinking about what was going to happen in the Savold fight to-night, but of what a great fighter Joe Louis was . . . and what a fine guy. For seventeen years he had fought the best fighters in the world. He had worn the supreme crown with dignity and power from 1937 until he retired undefeated champion in the spring of 1949 . . . twelve years in which he had proved himself the greatest ambassador of goodwill the coloured folk have had.

Joe Louis was not only a great fighter . . . he will always remain the greatest in my memory . . . but he was, and is, a good man. Throughout his career he kept his word, told the truth, and fought cleanly. He never abused his position, and while he was on friendly terms with white acquaintances, he chose his intimate friends from his own race. Louis would not tolerate racial outbursts. He never normally looked for trouble himself, and while he would not sit back and listen to any sneers at the expense of his people, he was just and would not stand for coloured folk's prejudices against whites. For a man who possessed so much violence in his fists he was a tolerant and timid man outside the ropes.

The Louis story begins at Lexington, Alabama on May 13, 1914, when a son was born to Monroe and Lillie Barrow who worked on a none too prosperous cotton farm. The boy was baptised Joseph Louis Barrow. He showed no inclination to fight until he was around sixteen. In fact, the big young coloured boy showed more inclination to use his hands on a violin or piano than in a boxing ring at an early age.

His father, a giant, died when Joe was a kid. His mother married a widower and the combined families moved on to Detroit where young Joe Barrow first showed signs of his ring greatness at the famous Brewster Centre Gymnasium.

Louis's trust in God was instilled at an early age by his mother, who insisted all her children should go to church and should always tell the truth.

It was her influence on him in his tenderest years that was

146

stamped on this big and simple fellow at the height of his career, for Joe Louis at no time lost his head.

His simplicity and sincerity humbled American stage, screen and political celebrities one night early in 1942 when 18,000 packed Madison Square Garden for a tournament in aid of the U.S. Navy Relief Society. They gave their speeches . . . some brilliant, some funny, some boring, but all were accepted in the right spirit, because America was united as the result of Japan's treacherous attack on Pearl Harbour a few months earlier.

Then they announced "Joe Louis, the heavyweight champion of the world." Louis, dressed as a G.I., went to the mike and, looking at the great crowd, said simply: "We've all got to do our part, and then we'll win. 'Cos we're on God's side."

A hush came over the crowd for a few seconds, and then cheering and clapping broke out. Some tough men gulped back as lumps rose in their throats. A few women present had tears in their eyes.

The sincerity of Joe Louis touched the hearts of America that night. And the sincerity of Joe touched the hearts of anybody who knew him. Not once did he make a statement before or after a fight that he did not mean. He praised or condemned opponents as he thought just, and while he was never boastful he did not hide behind a mock-screen of false modesty. If he won well, he said he was good. When he was bad, he admitted it.

His mother was responsible for his decision to become a fighter. She hadn't wanted it that way, but when Joe told her that was what he most wanted, she told him kindly: "Do what you want Joe, but if you're going to be a boxer make certain you're a *GOOD* one." Joe kept his word.

Louis learned his stuff at the Brewster Centre, but was beaten in his first amateur bout in 1932 by a Detroit light-heavyweight, Johnny Miler, who succeeded in flooring Joe seven times, but couldn't keep him down.

One of the remarkable things about Louis was that he learned something every time he went in the ring. The first lesson he learned from Miler was that you can't become a champion with one big punch. You've got to have science also. So he went back to the gym, and learned to jab with his left and make openings for his powerful right. All through his career Louis never made the same mistake twice. Schmeling had knocked him out to bring about his first professional defeat. He massacred the German in the return fight. Bob Pastor, Arturo Godoy, Tommy Farr and Jersey Joe Walcott took him the distance. He met them all again except Farr, and he knocked all three out in return bouts.

Louis was not invincible as an amateur, but he lost only four out of fifty-eight bouts. The majority of his victories were k.o's., and he went on to win the Golden Gloves title in 1934 beating a good amateur, Stanley Evans, who had licked him a year earlier.

In the summer of 1934 he turned professional under the managership of John Roxburgh and Julian Black, and under the care and attention of Jack Blackburn, the trainer, and himself a useful fighter many years earlier.

Louis's professional career began sensationally. He was only just twenty. Yet before he was 21 he had won all his 22 pro. bouts, 18 of them by knockouts. Soon after he became of age he was matched with Carnera, and knocked out the former world heavyweight champion in 6 rounds. After this, top performers like King Levinsky, Max Baer, Paolino Uzcudun and Charlie Retzlaff were all knocked out. Now nothing stood between this young Brown Bomber and the heavyweight championship . . . except Max Schmeling, the German who had once held the title, but had lost it to Jack Sharkey four years earlier.

Schmeling was campaigning to regain the crown which was now in the hands of Jim Braddock. The young Negro began a favourite against the hard-hitting German, but Schmeling that June night in 1936 battered Louis to defeat in 12 rounds. The young coloured fighter, in spite of his fine record, was still raw and was a complete sucker as Schmeling actually led with right swings which smashed Louis down and finally ended the fight. But at least Louis had shown his guts.

Within two months of this hiding, Louis was back knocking out Sharkey in three rounds, until one year later he went into the ring and won the world heavyweight crown from Braddock by an 8-round k.o.

Schmeling naturally considered he had been given a raw deal —as, in fact, he had. But then any relation between American boxing politics and justice is purely accidental.

Louis's first defence of his title was against Tommy Farr, and it is a credit to the Welsh heavyweight that the Brown Bomber failed to stop him after 15 fierce rounds. Schmeling was given his chance in 1938. Louis, normally a fighter without hatred in his heart, hated Schmeling that night. The German, who was a supporter of Hitler and his Nazi regime, had said many unkind things about Joe. Also Joe's pride—and he has a very strong pride—had been hurt by the only knockout defeat he had ever suffered. Furthermore, Joe hadn't forgotten that in the first fight Schmeling had hit him after the bell.

It was murder this time. Louis didn't even sit on his stool before the fight began. He stood in his corner hopping on first one foot and then the other. He couldn't get at Schmeling soon enough. When the gong sounded, he rushed from his corner and threw three left jabs at the German's face. Schmeling, remembering his success with his right in their first meeting, now led with a right but was short with it.

This was Louis's chance. He let go with his own right, and the black-browed German landed on the ropes. The angry Louis followed up with a vicious right to the body, and the German let out a dreadful cry. This was all Louis wanted to know he had Schmeling beaten. The next minute was legalised slaughter. Louis dropped Schmeling twice with good punches to the jaw, and as the German, already licked, turned his back on the champion on the ropes, Louis slammed him in the kidneys. This was not a foul and had no bearing on the result. Schmeling was already beaten before this punch landed, and

149

when a fighter turns his back on his opponent, he—and not the deliverer of the blow—is responsible for where it lands.

Schmeling squealed afterwards, went to hospital and was carried off the ship at Hamburg on a stretcher. I guess he had to make the most of any excuse because Hitler had made elaborate plans to welcome Herr Max back to Germany as the heavyweight champion of the world. His complete execution in less than $2\frac{1}{2}$ minutes of fighting was humiliating for Schmeling and embarrassing for his Fuhrer.

Louis continued to bowl over the best opposition available, and then war came. He had one scare when Billy Conn, a former light-heavyweight champion and a brilliant boxer, nearly dethroned him in 1941. Conn led all the way until the thirteenth round. By this time Billy had become cocky, underrating Joe's punching power. The Brown Bomber waited for this to happen, and with the first mistake Billy made he was knocked flat.

I flew out to New York for the return Conn fight in the summer of 1946. This fight was ballyhooed to be equivalent to the Dempsey-Carpentier championship after the first world war. Mike Jacobs forecast that it would draw 3,000,000 dollars. He charged 100 dollars for the ringside. His target was not reached, but nevertheless, 45,000 fans paid 1,925,564 dollars—second-largest receipts on boxing after the 2,658,000 dollars paid to see the second Dempsey-Tunney fight.

As a fight it flopped. I had got to know both Joe Louis and Billy Conn pretty well while they were serving in the American Forces in Britain. Conn had softened up with the war years. He had a pretty swell time in this country, and although he bluffed his way right through training, Billy must have realised he was in for a beating. Every bit of confidence drained from him the day before the fight.

I had spent much time with him at Greenwood Lake in New Jersey, and was shaken by his sudden change. He was a white-faced fighter the night he entered the Yankee Stadium ring, and his performance was pathetic. All his earlier boasts were forgotten. He back-pedalled from Louis for eight rounds without throwing a serious punch or winning a round.

Joe, still a superb fighter in 1946, moved in at the eighth round and with that lightning right-hand punch to the jaw knocked Billy flat. The Irish boy from Pittsburgh didn't make any attempt to rise.

Conn never fought again, after collecting his share of the purse which was £75,000. Louis picked up over £150,000 that night for one of his easiest fights. Conn was lucky to get out as a young man of 28 with plenty of money. He was still luckier when a friend advised him to put his fortune into oil, with the result that to-day Billy Conn is probably the richest ex-boxer outside of Gene Tunney.

I saw Louis knockout Jersey Joe Walcott in 11 rounds at Yankee Stadium in June, 1948. Old Man Jersey Joe had given a Louis who was now falling to pieces a scare at Madison Square Garden in December 1947, flooring him a couple of times. Even Joe thought he had lost his title that night, but the judges gave Louis the decision.

As usual, Joe learned by his first mistake. Walcott was again giving him a boxing lesson in the second fight for 10 rounds, but Joe was stalking Jersey Joe who had succeeded in dropping the champ for a count in the third round. Louis saw his chance in the eleventh. He still could whip over that right. Walcott was down and out before he knew what had hit him.

Louis went on a long exhibition tour after this, not taking part in any further contests. He announced his retirement in March 1949. I wish he had stayed retired, but in spite of the fact that his total earnings were near the 5,000,000 dollar mark, Joe found himself short of ready cash in 1950. Much of his earnings had been invested in real estate and in annuities which would not be realised for some years later. And he was in plenty of trouble with Uncle Sam's tax inspectors.

Joe had been under the impression that many of his contracts with Mike Jacobs included a settlement of tax, but this did not prove to be the case. His earnings had ceased with the war and so, to my deep regret, Louis decided to hit the come-back trail in September, 1950, against Ezzard Charles, who had won the N.B.A. version of the world heavyweight championship with a dull victory over Jersey Joe Walcott. The New York State Athletic Commission agreed to recognise the winner of the Louis-Charles battle as world champion.

I flew once more to New York for this battle. Louis had looked sluggish at his Pompton Lakes camp, but had come to life in the last couple of days so that I dared not pick again this man who I regarded as a king of the ring. So often had I seen him defy all the odds and win through with one punch. But it was not to be so this night.

The lion had lost its claws. The tiger had lost its spring, and a pathetic Joe Louis, his reflexes gone, was outboxed and out-jabbed by a workmanlike but not a brilliant champion. Only once did Joe nearly win the fight. This was in the 10th round when he staggered Charles with one of his old right handers. Ezzard staggered for a split second. The old Louis would have struck again with the speed of a cobra, but it just wasn't there anymore, and Charles took a comfortable decision.

Louis admitted to me in the dressing room afterwards he no longer had what it takes, yet he must have believed he could do better because he didn't announce his retirement but went on fighting—beating men like Cesar Brion, Freddie Beshore and Omelio Agremonte twice. And so to the meeting with Lee Savold in June, 1951. Once more I was to take the Clipper to New York to see my idol of the ring perform. Joe was now 37, yet still few of the experts dared to tip against him, and certainly not this writer. Savold, after all, wasn't any chicken himself. He was, in fact, only one year younger than Joe at 36.

Savold could never be classed at any time with Louis, but Lee had become a changed man since his long stay in England where he had shattered Bruce Woodcock six months earlier at London's White City in a bout which Jack Solomons advertised as a world heavyweight title fight and to which the British

152

Boxing Board of Control were foolish enough to give their blessing. We knew in our hearts the winner could never seriously be called world champion until he had beaten either Ezzard Charles or Joe Louis.

Savold, a former playboy, cut out his cigar-smoking and beer-guzzling habits while in England. He reduced a flabby stomach, and began all over again with a new ambition. "In America they treated me like a bum so I behaved like one," Lee explained to me one night. "The British have treated me like a gentleman and I want to act like one. I wish I had come to England ten years earlier."

It was in this mood that Savold was going into this Louis fight. I had spent some days with him at his camp at South Fallsburg in the Catskills, and no fighter had trained with more endeavour. He honestly believed he could take this 1951 edition of Louis who was heavier than at any time in his career.

The fight should have taken place in New York's Polo Grounds, but two nights of rain had seen it postponed until the Friday, and it had been transferred to Madison Square Garden.

It was a big and ponderous Louis who climbed into the ring that night, but Savold was tailor-made for the old Brown Bomber, and Joe temporarily recaptured some of the old Black Magic that had taken him to the top of the heavyweight tree nearly fifteen years earlier. Savold was disappointing. He didn't bob and weave—a style that had always puzzled Joe, but stood up straight and became a standing target for Joe's left jabs. From the second round onwards blood poured from Lee's nose. He kept feinting as though he was about to do something, but only once did he follow up with a sharp right. This was at the beginning of the fourth round, and Joe's right eye began to puff up immediately.

But Lee was chopped round the ring in the fifth, and again in the sixth. Louis forced him on to the ropes, and with one of his old lightning right hooks softened the Minnesota cowboy for the vicious left hook that was whipped across. Savold went down as though coshed. He struggled to get up, but couldn't do it.

So convincing was the old man Joe Louis that the experts forgot his defeat by Ezzard Charles, and began saying that he might after all become the first fighter in history to regain the world heavyweight title in his second attempt at a come-back.

But it was not to be. Had Louis fought a return with Charles as he was promised he may have regained the crown. But in the meantime, Charles unexpectedly lost his crown to Jersey Joe Walcott, and Louis was persuaded to take on the tough up-and-coming undefeated Brockton heavyweight, Rocky Marciano, with the winner fighting for the title.

Marciano had chopped up Savold a few months earlier, and although he was undefeated they said he was crude and still a novice. He hadn't been able to finish Savold off with one punch. It had taken intervention of the referee to end the fight. And so once again most of the boxing writers strung along with Louis, but the Brown Bomber had finally hit the end of the trail . . . after 17 glorious years. He had given as much as he had taken for seven rounds, and had cut Marciano's nose and eyes, but then the murderous-punching Marciano, ten years the younger fighter, had pushed Louis on to the ropes and with a left and right to the jaw had sent Joe crashing through the ropes to lay unconscious outside. Referee Ruby Goldstein did not even start to count. Instead he stopped the fight as Joe lay helpless. It was a knockout win for Rocky—and only the second time in Joe's career—but Ruby didn't want the task of tolling the fatal 10 over this great Black Prince of the Ring.

But I have run on too far. I should have stopped after Louis's temporary come-back triumph over Lee Savold. We are back in Dempsey's after Savold's defeat. It is in the early hours of the next morning, and many of the boys are forecasting that Louis is going to win back the title when one of the boys ribs Kearns again: "Who d'ya like—Dempsey or Louis?" he asks with a grin.

Kearns was speaking up again. "If the finest fighter of them

154

all, Jack Dempsey, couldn't do it, Louis won't do it" snapped the old Doc. "I tell you the guys that Louis beat were just bums. He don't rate with Dempsey."

I did not argue any more. I let Kearns have his way. Louis never regained his crown. Perhaps the Doc was also right about Louis and Dempsey. I know that if I am spared as long as the Doc, I shall in all sincerity tell younger listeners that there never will be another heavyweight like Joe Louis. I wasn't privileged to see Dempsey in action.

CHAPTER IV

TURPIN'S FATEFUL "RIDE" TO NEW YORK

RANDOLPH ADOLPHUS TURPIN, wide-eyed and dusky son of a West Indian father and white mother, was born with more natural fistic ability than any champion produced in these Isles for thirty years. Like Jimmy Wilde, he was created with the skill to punch correctly. Unlike Wilde, Randolph was blessed with perfect physique . . . those supple brown muscles would have been the envy of Hercules. Pound for pound he hit harder at his best than any British fighter I saw, including Eric Boon, a devastating punching lightweight.

Turpin clutched at greatness when he reached his peak that night in July 1951 at Earls Court, London, when, with as dead-pan a mask as a learned judge about to pronounce yet another death sentence, he outboxed, outjabbed and outpunched Sugar Ray Robinson to bring the world middleweight title to Britain. But his triumph did something to him, because never again did he box or fight so well. He never regained the fitness and sharpness. Neither was he ever so clear of eye or so mentally relaxed and content. Randy reigned as a world king for but sixty-four days before Robinson took back the crown which the Americans chaffed was just another article in "lease-lend" to Britain.

I criticise Turpin because he was born with every physical asset a fighter could possess. Yet his mental outlook as far as being a world champion was sadly lacking. To enjoy a lengthy reign on a golden but envied and precarious throne a pugilist must possess determination, ambition and responsibility. He cannot shrug his shoulders, throw a friendly grin and adopt a couldn't-care-less attitude. He must be a killer; he must hate, and be for ever aware of the fact that the moment he relaxes either inside or outside the ring there are a dozen or more hungry pugilists waiting to slap him down.

A champion, of course, must always be fit, whether or not he has a fight on hand. But he must also have a burning ambition to remain top-dog. Take Harry Greb, one of the world's greatest middleweights. Harry was a playboy, but he remained a superb fighter until inevitably his gay life caught up with him. Harry was ambitious, determined and courageous. He loved fighting for the sake of it. He had the killer instinct, possessed a burning pride, could hate, and would fight for nothing if he thought his fistic reputation was being challenged.

Turpin's outlook on life is more easy-going. Had he the determination of, say, Tommy Farr, he could have held his head high in the company of such middleweight champions as Fitzsimmons, Stanley Ketchel, Harry Greb, Mickey Walker and Sugar Robinson. In fact, he could have outshone them all. That he hasn't—and never will in my opinion—is his own fault.

I shall never forget my trip to America in the late summer of 1953 when Turpin was to do battle with Carl "Bobo" Olson, a fighter born in Honolulu of a Swedish father and Portuguese mother. This match was to settle once and for all the world middleweight championship which had become vacant following the retirement of Robinson. Olson had won the American title, and Turpin had made it clear he was still the best middleweight in Europe by outboxing Charles Humez of France. A more fantastic preparation for a world championship battle I never did see ,and the more I look back on it the more amazed I am. If ever a pugilist threw away a chance of a million dollars it was Randy Turpin who, from the day he sailed in the *Queen Mary* in August, gave us all the impression that he couldn't care less what the future held.

Turpin had begun to slip from the time he was so magnificent in victory over Robinson. After being stopped by Sugar in the return, his performances became more and more disappointing.

He was ring-rusty against Alex Buxton, George Angelo and other opponents. Not only did he seem to have lost his big punch, but his attitude was indifferent. He seemed content to outbox his opponents. The old killer instinct of his amateur and early professional days had gone. He remained a clever boxer, but the old black magic was no more.

This went on up to the Humez fight in the summer of 1953. Randy had seldom visited London or even his native Leamington. Most of his time was spent at Abergele in North Wales, where he lived in a castle. It came as a big shock, therefore, when, at the weigh-in against Humez, Turpin was overweight, and only after being rushed to a turkish baths by Jack Solomons did he make the necessary 11st. 6 lbs. in the hour allowed him.

Whatever excuses Randy offered, he still had no right to come in overweight for such an important fight, which the British Boxing Board of Control claimed to be for the vacant world championship. That clearly was a sign of Turpin's lack of responsibility to himself, the promoter and the British public. His old trainer, Bill Hyman, had already parted company with the camp, and Randy began to supervise his own training . . . that he was not capable of doing this efficiently was more painfully clear in the fateful Olson fight that followed.

So tense and on edge did the British boy become that long before the fight with Olson was due he had exchanged cross words with everybody including Solomons, his manager, his brothers, the British and American boxing writers. His camp at Grossinger's in the Catskill Mountains was the unhappiest I have ever visited, although for myself I must confess Randy was not once unpleasant or offhand to me. Before this trip, few folk realised Turpin is deaf in one ear, and this certainly accounted for some misunderstandings. Two American sports writers, for example, were under the impression Randy was giving them the cold shoulder. "He didn't hear your questions," I said, as they began to accuse him of being a son-of-a-gun. "Move round the other side, and he'll hear you." They took my advice, and Turpin answered every question in a friendly fashion.

However, it can't be denied that Randy didn't like certain members of the Press, and usually locked himself up if he saw them coming first. Neither could it be denied Turpin was moody and sometimes morose. He admitted he missed his girl, Gwen Price, who lived near the Welsh castle. They were married soon after his return from America.

Randolph certainly hasn't any reason to be unfriendly with the boxing writers. He owes quite a bit to some of us, because I still have a letter written to me before the war by George Middleton. This letter contains an appeal by Middleton on behalf of Randolph's brother, Dick, who had beaten some of the best middleweights around, but could not get championship recognition because of a British Boxing Board of Control regulation which barred a coloured fighter. A good middleweight from Manchester, Len Johnson, had never been allowed to take part in a title bout because of this undemocratic rule.

Middleton pleaded with me to give Dick Turpin my support. He pointed out that the boy's father, a West Indian, had served Britain with the King's Royal Rifles in the first world war. That he had been gassed in France, and discharged. As a result of bad health, he died a comparatively young man leaving a white widow and five children . . . the youngest being a dusky baby boy of nine months named Randolph. I took up the Turpin cause and ran a "Scrap the Colour Bar" campaign. I could not at first get any real support, but continued the crusade. Later, I was able to point out that a good middleweight from the West Indies, Stafford Barton, died in action while serving with the R.A.F. as an air-gunner in the second world war. That another West Indian welterweight, Lefty "Satan" Flynn, served in the Merchant Navy. That Dick Turpin had joined the Army, Jackie Turpin was on convoys and that young Randolph had become a cook in the Royal Navy.

The heading I ran that "Coloured Boys could die for Britain

but not fight for a British championship" caused considerable comment, and the situation was taken up in a big way after the war by John Lewis, who was then a Socialist M.P. for Bolton, and a keen boxing fan. Lewis pressed the matter with the Colonial Office, and I dined with him and a Government official when the matter was thoroughly discussed. Not long afterwards, the Boxing Board revised their regulations ending the unjust colour bar.

The first boxer to benefit was Dick Turpin, who made boxing history by becoming the first coloured fighter ever to win a British title when he defeated Vince Hawkins in 1948. Dick's kid brother Randolph had also set up a record by being the first coloured boy to win an A.B.A. title, and Randolph later lifted the professional title, knocking out Albert Finch, who had taken the crown off Dick. So, generally speaking, the Turpins haven't had such a bad deal from the British Press.

Randy wasn't at his physical peak against Olson. He argued afterwards that he went fifteen rounds and, therefore, must have been fit, but I disagree with him. Turpin was but a shadow of his old self, and only went 15 rounds by leaning back on the ropes for long periods of the bout. Some reporters tried to make a mystery of his tactics, declaring that had he moved round the ring like the old Randy instead of staying put and taking punishment, he must have won. I don't believe his legs were strong enough to enable him to attack for 15 rounds. He stayed the distance only by the strange but necessary tactics adopted. My own belief that he was not as physically perfect as two years earlier was confirmed by Dr. Vincent Nardiello, New York State Athletic Commission medical officer, who examined him before both fights.

I have said that one big mistake was for Randy to spend so many weeks in America before the fight. Certainly, another shocking error he made was to appoint himself as dictator of the training camp. Randy boxed just when he liked and, in fact, did everything just as he pleased. I motored to Grossinger's three times, but he never boxed at any of these visits.

TOMMY FARR—THE TONYPANDY KID

Black Dynamite! Joe Louis, with anger in his heart, shows what a perfect executioner he is when battering Max Schmeling to defeat in the 1st round of their world-title clash in 1938. In 1936 Schmeling had inflicted Louis's first-ever defeat when he battered the young Brown Bomber in 12 rounds. Neither boxer was champion in the first meeting.

Instead he was concentrating on long walks to build up his legs to stay the distance, but as Randy was ring-rusty at the Humez fight he needed more than anything else boxing . . . plenty of boxing.

I did see him spar four rounds five days before the fight. He was due to go two rounds each with three opponents. He looked like the old Turpin in the first round. The second session was O.K., but in the third and fourth rounds he looked tired, and his arms had dropped low. When the third opponent stepped in to give Randy a fifth and sixth round, the British champion waved him away. Neither Middleton nor Algar were consulted. Neither protested. How can a fighter in preparation for a world championship hope to succeed if he isn't prepared to go six rounds in training?

Turpin didn't box many rounds throughout his whole training spell, and this finally convinced me he did not have a chance against Olson and I cabled my column to the *News of the World* reporting how unhappy I was about his strange approach to a fight which if he won could have been worth a million dollars to him. An annoyed Jack Solomons kept away from the camp for ten days before the fight, and Teddy Waltham, British Boxing Board of Control secretary, made two special journeys for the purpose of giving Randy pep talks on just how important it was for British boxing that he should win this fight.

But Turpin remained unstirred. He was without weight difficulties. If anything he was too light at 11 st. 3 lbs. at the midday weigh-in. Randy is not a great reader of books, but he thrives on comics. As I came through the main entrance of Madison Square Garden, about one hour before Randy was due in the ring, I met Harry Markson of the International Boxing Club. Harry was amused. He had just arranged with the doorman to allow Algar, the trainer, to be passed out in order to buy a fresh supply of American comics for Randy.

The fight itself turned out to be one of the poorest world championships I ever saw. Olson is just a strong fellow who throws hundreds of punches, but not always accurately. He had twice lost to Sugar Ray Robinson and twice to Dave Sands. The old Turpin would have battered him. Olson is not a big puncher, and many of his blows against Turpin were cuffs delivered with the inside of the glove.

Turpin, realising he would have to win quickly or lose, ran from his corner like a young man in a hurry and gave Olson everything he had for three rounds. Left hooks to head and body, and rights, were thrown from all angles. It was a desperate gamble that might have come off. Olson was punched round the ring like a novice, but he was game and took everything the British champion threw at him. Some ringsiders thought Randy had pulled a great bluff in his training and had conditioned himself secretly, but most of us knew this was not the case. Had the old Turpin thrown as many blows, Olson would have been down and out, but the snap wasn't there any more.

Randy suddenly ran out of gas. I had expected this, but not so soon. Yet those opening rounds had exposed Olson as a moderate but game champion. He had not revealed a K.O. punch. Yet he was able to put Turpin down for a count of 5 in the ninth and 9 in the tenth. It was not the power of his blows so much as Turpin's own weakness that caused the British champion to go down in the ninth. A succession of left and right swings to the British boy's head did the damage. Turpin looked a sorry picture with blood pouring from a cut below his left eye, and more blood from his mouth. He was still down at 5 when the bell sounded the end of the round, and a weary fighter dragged himself to his corner.

Throughout the tenth round he continued to rest on the ropes in an upright position with his chin a perfect target for the flapping lefts and rights of Bobo. A left to the head dropped Turpin for 9, but had Olson possessed a knockout blow the British champion would have been pole-axed. The fight continued its dreary way. Randy lacked strength, Olson had stamina but no punch, and so we watched the British champion losing many of the rounds, but knowing that had he been anywhere near his old self Olson could not have beaten him. An infuriating and frustrating experience for any British boxing writer to experience.

By the last round, Olson's own fire had died and he, like Turpin, was tired. To Randy's credit, he rallied sufficiently to take this round, but although he threw wild and desperate blows there was nothing there to upset Olson, who burst into tears when he was declared an undisputed winner. I must pass comment here on the inconsistency of the American system of scoring. The referee, Al Berl, awarded 9 rounds to Olson, 4 to Turpin and 2 even. Judge Suskind gave Olson 8 rounds, Turpin 7 and Judge Shortell awarded Olson 11 and Turpin 4. I scored Olson 7, Turpin 4 and 4 even. For those interested in figures, 18,969 paid $167,651 ($132,455 net). T.V. and radio realised $60,000, and each fighter received 30 per cent. of an overall net of $189,445 which meant about $56,835 each.

Turpin had also disappointed two years earlier when he lost his world title back to Robinson at the Yankee Stadium. He was a fitter and stronger fighter than the one who was to lose to Olson, but he was not the same Turpin who had beaten Robinson in London nine weeks earlier. It wasn't lack of condition that caused his defeat this time, but the failure of himself and his corner to handle a crisis. He had boxed calmly if not brilliantly for nine rounds, and Robinson was blowing up just as sure as night follows day. Nobody in the Yankee Stadium that night realised more than Sugar himself that if the fight lasted another two or three rounds only Turpin would be standing up.

The tenth round was half-way through when the Leamington Licker split open Sugar's left eye. It now looked a million to one on the English boy, but Randy, wide of eye, blank of expression, was not even moved by the sight of blood, a sight that should have inspired him to beat a victory roll on Robinson's head. Instead, he committed the unforgivable sin, breaking the first commandment of pugilism which says:

"Thou shalt not forget to defend thyself at ALL times." For a split second, Randolph dropped his hands to his side. That was sufficient an opening for a fighter as experienced as the Sugar Boy. A second earlier, the Harlem Negro's eyes had flashed out panic as he thumbed away the blood that dripped from the deep gash. He had looked as desperate as a man trapped by fire in a locked room on the third floor of a building. Turpin unlocked a window for him. Sugar did the obvious by gambling on a jump. He had everything to gain, and nothing to lose. The gamble came off as in that split second he threw everything he had into as desperate a right swing as I have ever seen. Turpin, usually so intelligent in defence, stood there and took it as though it had been made to measure.

The next second the Leamington lad was stretched on his back, almost out. He showed his courage by rising and refusing to take another count although he was smacked twenty or thirty times, and was swaying on the ropes, but still managing to ride many of Robinson's wild swings which were beginning to lose their power, when the referee stepped in and stopped the fight with only 8 seconds of the tenth round remaining. Until the official intervened, Robinson had become as desperate again as before he threw that one big right. All his efforts to annihilate the British boy seemed to have failed, and he himself was now physically washed up from his own exertions. He was breathing heavily, and was incapable of keeping up the flurry of punches he had begun to throw when Turpin first took refuge on the ropes. Relief suddenly appeared in his eyes though when Ruby Goldstein stepped in and stopped the bout. He found sufficient energy to smile and do a little victory jig.

I was disappointed in both New York fights because the Americans never saw the real Turpin. Only Nat Fleischer, Editor of *The Ring* magazine, knows, because Nat saw Turpin in plenty of fights in England when he was at his best, and Nat had warned Sugar Robinson not to take the English boy too lightly. Robinson forgot this advice, and had a gay old time in Paris before the fight. Throughout history there have been examples of the ring kings failing in their attempts to cheat nature by burning the candle at both ends. Yet few pugilists benefit from the lessons of predecessors. I don't suppose the young fighter will ever learn—until it is too late.

What does the future hold for Turpin? He is still young, and, at the time of writing, good enough to beat most European middleweights. I don't believe, however, we shall ever again see the Randy who lifted British boxing to the skies with his brilliant win over Robinson. My only regret is that Randy himself didn't realise how great he might have been.

CHAPTER V

THE KING WHO CHOSE TO BE CLOWN-PRINCE

THE OUTSTANDING KINGS of the ring have been mostly moulded from sober-minded athletes, ferocious of mood, dead-pan of expression. Corbett, Fitzsimmons, Jeffries, Burns, Dempsey, Tunney and Louis took their profession as seriously as any surgeon engaged in a theatre where life or death is the stake. And Rocky Marciano, the present ruler of the heavyweight division, regards the fight game as a grim business which is a full-time job, but that the reward is well worth the effort. Jack Johnson was one of the few exceptions, because Lil' Arthur stands out both as an all-time great and as a playboy. Harry Greb also is in the running, but his fame was never so international as Johnson's.

Normally, we expect our pugilistic idols to take their fighting in a businesslike fashion, yet what a dull, dull ring it would be if the occasional character, the buffoon, the champ who breaks all the rules and gets away with it, did not appear on the fistic horizon to relieve a tense situation, just like the circus clown who arrives to help the audience to relax once more after they have become keyed up by an exciting death leap in a trapeze act.

These characters make good copy for the sporting columnists, they amuse the fight fans, and, while some of them are not exactly the type we would want to leave our wives alone with, wouldn't the fight game be less glamorous and less colourful, and wouldn't our memories be less light-hearted, when we try to escape from looking back on only the bloody, tragic, and hard-luck stories of the ring?

We have all laughed at Max Baer, Maxie Rosenbloom, Two-

166

Ton Tony Galento, Kingfish Levinsky and his sister "Leaping Lena," and Pat Comiskey. We have at times almost despaired of Jack Doyle, and Lee Oma nearly caused English fans to weep with his antics in the Woodcock fight. But they have all brought their share of blood, sweat, laughter and tears to the prize ring.

Max Baer was by far the best of the ring buffoons. I don't mean Max was the most successful clown, but that he was the most impressive heavyweight who ever chose to be a funny man. Baer, in fact, only missed by a wise-crack going into the list of the truly great heavyweights. As it is, he will still go down in my memory as the best of the big fellows outside of Joe Louis, allowing for the fact that Rocky Marciano may yet improve sufficiently to leave first Baer and then Louis behind him.

Baer did win the world heavyweight title—although he only held that glamorous crown for one year. He was the biggest puncher I saw—an opinion that Tommy Farr, who fought him twice, vouches from personal experience, having fought 27 rounds with Baer . . . and if Tommy couldn't find that out in eighty-one minutes of throwing and taking punches, nobody else ever will.

Had Baer not been born with such a screwball sense of humour, or had Nature provided him with the calculating-machine brain of Tunney or the love of fighting for the sake of fighting that burned in the heart of Dempsey, Maxie would have lined up with the Corbetts, Fitzsimmons and Dempseys. He had the physique of a Greek god, the strength of Hercules and the occasional fury of a jungle beast. And he was born with a trip-hammer in his right fist.

But for all these gifts which the average heavyweight prays for, Baer seemed more content to be the great lover rather than the great glover. The ladies loved him, and he loved the ladies to love him, and he didn't care who knew it. He was, for instance, delighted with the American sports columnist who dedicated these limericks to him:

167

There was a young scrapper named Baer
Who had the most beautiful hair;
He could flirt, he could fight,
He could dance all the night,
That fantastic fast-puncher, Max Baer!

That frivolous fighter named Baer
Had the ladies all up in the air,
He would love 'em and leave 'em,
And blithely deceive 'em,
That bewitching young biffer, Max Baer!

Maxie possessed the oddest sense of humour. Even in the middle of a bloody battle, he would suddenly see the funny side of the situation, and would start grinning and wise-cracking at his opponent, who seldom appreciated a joke when his head was singing, his arms aching and his nose bleeding.

What, for instance, can you say about a character who when undergoing a physical examination at the Commission Office prior to his world championship bout with Carnera, plucked hairs from the giant's chest and wisecracked: "He loves me, he loves me not!"; and who, when he tripped over Carnera in the second round after dropping him, is alleged to have quipped: "Come on, Primo, last up's a cissy!"

After this, he put on an act of clowning, frowning, sneering, jeering to cover up the fact that he wasn't in too good condition physically, but, at the same time, he floored Carnera eleven times before reducing the Italian Alp to a battered and bleeding victim. Baer looked like a splendid champion in spite of his comedy act in winning the world title, but because of his playboy antics and inconsistency he failed even to approach mediocrity one year later when he lost his title to an opponent whose chance of success was 10 to 1 against in the betting. It was certainly a golden opportunity for Jim Braddock, a veteran and modest heavyweight, who earlier had been forced to go on the dole to provide food for his wife and family. Even Braddock must have been astonished by Baer's novice-like performance.

England saw the same "Jekyll and Hyde" character of Max Baer. When he arrived in London in the spring of 1937 to tackle Tommy Farr, most of the boxing writers were talking of massacre. Farr had just won the British heavyweight title from Ben Foord in a scrappy bout, but still had not won the affection of the British fight crowd.

Baer had one of his off-nights. He began scowling, grinning and pulling faces enough to frighten off the horrible child, but such tactics were a waste of time against the dour Welshman who wasn't afraid of anything on two legs—or on four, for that matter. Tommy Bach, as confident as Tarzan in the jungle, just poked out a spitfire left hand, split open Baer's brow, and walked away with the decision after 12 rounds to the delight of thousands of his countrymen who stood and sang their national anthem with a fervour that only the Welsh can put to song.

Yet it was quite a different Baer who crushed Ben Foord in nine rounds at Harringay six weeks later. I have a clear picture of the end as Baer let go with a terrible right which missed the South African's chin by inches. Like lightning, Max brought his right fist back and shattered Foord with the back of his fist and quickly followed up with a terrific left swing. This all happened so rapidly that not more than a few ringsiders could have seen it, although Baer risked disqualification with his speedy backhander. Foord looked in a bad way for a little while, and Maxie was concerned until Ben recovered and left the ring apparently none the worse for his shattering experience.

The Tommy Farr who met Baer again in New York a year later also experienced a different opponent to the one he met in England. Max, realising he was not fighting a mug as he had been misled to believe before the first fight, really hammered tough Tommy, dropping him with a murderous right. It was only Farr's courage and toughness that kept him going for 15 rounds.

What then is behind the queer streak in this Glamour Boy of the Ring who, on his night, had the beating of any heavyweight in the world, but on his off-nights fought worse than a bum?

The American public probably saw Max at his greatest the night he battered Max Schmeling, former world heavyweight champion, to defeat in ten rounds 'way back in 1933. This was a bout between the two hardest right-hand hitters of their day, but the young Baer finally hammered Schmeling into submission. But why in the tenth round did the Playboy turned Killer hold back a final right that would have put the helpless German out for minutes—or longer?

Perhaps here we now discover the psychological reason why Baer just missed walking alongside the immortals of the prize ring. Why he developed into the Pranker of Prankers. And why, under pressure from Joe Louis, he showed a streak that suggested he didn't really like the fight game . . . in that bout he was counted out quite conscious but shaking his head as he knelt on the canvas.

We have to go back some way to find some reason why Baer wasn't the complete heavyweight champion. He was born in Omaha, Nebraska. His grandfather was a German-Jew, and his mother had Scottish blood in her. Jacob Baer, his father, kept a slaughter-house. When Max was thirteen the family moved to Livermore, California, where his dad took over a slaughter-house and cattle ranch of his own. The youngster followed his father's steps and, no doubt, helped to develop that terrific right-hand wallop from his early efforts with a pole-axe.

At twenty Baer was a handsome six-footer of thirteen and a half stone, but not interested in the fight game or in the girls. But at twenty-one he was encouraged to have his first bout with an Indian named Chief Cariboo. The redskin was scalped in a couple of rounds.

Baer quickly ran up a score of K.O. successes and was making a big name in California when he stepped in with Frankie Campbell at San Francisco in 1930. Campbell was a more experienced fighter and a better boxer, and most folk thought Baer at last had been over-matched.

But after being behind on points, the Livermore Larruper managed to catch up with Campbell, and that terrible right began to chop down Frankie like it had cattle. In the fifth round Campbell collapsed from the terrible battering. Baer was cock-a-hoop, but not for long, because poor Campbell never regained consciousness, and Baer was charged with manslaughter.

Max was rightly cleared of the charge, but for some reason was suspended for one year by the California Boxing Commission, and was given quite a battering by many of the Californian sports writers who had a great regard for Campbell. What effect this tragedy had on the 21-year-old Californian can never be assessed, but he wasn't the same fighter for quite a time after. Ancil Hoffman, who had promoted the Campbell fight, became his manager and Baer was taken to New York where he lost a points decision to Ernie Schaaf. He did knockout Tom Heeney, but dropped decisions to Johnny Risko and Paolino Uzcudun before really settling down again to list a string of K.O. successes.

In 1932 he met Schaaf again in Chicago, and won a punishing ten-round fight. Six months later Schaaf collapsed in a tame bout with Carnera, and many boxing writers claimed Schaaf died as the result of the heavy head punishment sustained against Baer. Poor Maxie could not escape unfortunate publicity. Here he stood accused of being responsible for the death of two fighters. Is it to be wondered that Baer had a disliking at heart for the fight game? Is it to be wondered why he held back on Schmeling at the finish, and why he seemed startled when Foord went white? It must have been a relief every time he saw a K.O.'ed opponent come round! Is it even to be wondered why he wasn't too game against Joe Louis when his own head was singing from the Brown Bomber's right smashes?

Why then did Max Baer remain in the fight game for a dozen years? He knew no other profession where he could have earned half a million dollars, and it still held some glamour for him. From inside the ropes he could always switch an eye on some adoring blonde.

Possibly his playboy antics were a form of escapism, because

171

it was after the trouble over the Campbell tragedy that he first met Dorothy Dunbar at Reno late in 1930, and persuaded her to marry him the following July. Earlier he had fallen for a waitress named Olive Beck, and Baer had soon become favourite in a very tricky race known as the Casanova Stakes. The quiet shy good-looker from Livermore came out of his shell in a big way. And didn't the gals fall for this husky piece of manhood.

Baer went on a glorious round of clubs and cocktail parties. He boasted of a sixteen-cylinder Cadillac, and several mere "Straight-Eights." He was more relaxed amid the soft lights of night clubs than the sweaty atmosphere of the gymnasium, and preferred to beat the drums in a jazz band to beating an opponent's brains out. Maxie found it far more fun in a clinch with a blonde without a referee there to shout "Break!"

When he fought there were always enough dollies from the follies present in the first two rows of the ringside to fill a chorus, and Maxie thrived on their admiring glances.

It was all fun while it lasted, but Maxie wasn't the first man to discover Hell hath no fury as a woman scorned! Soon he was being chased by and chasing so many Hollywood beauties that a few began carrying their broken hearts into court, and Hollywood dedicated a signature tune especially for Baer. It's title was "I'll be sueing you!"

These affairs of the heart plus his love for extravagant cars and expensive parties helped Maxie to run through the best part of half a million dollars in ten years, but he isn't by any means hard up, because a fair portion of his earnings were wisely invested, and he has been reaping the steady benefit of this wisdom in recent years.

Dorothy Dunbar had hardly finished sueing him for divorce when his old waitress sweetheart, Olive, filed a breach of promise suit. He was then playing Cupid with June Knight, who was charming Broadway with her voice and ability to dance. Amid all this, his first manager, J. Hamilton, began legal action concerning one of his fights. But Maxie kept smiling.

172

Later he was to marry Mary Sullivan, a girl nothing to do with stage or Hollywood, and who certainly helped Max to settle down. She advised him to look after the cash he was earning with spilled blood and the £50,000 odd collected from the Louis fiasco was put into a trust fund which he has found welcome in recent years.

For all his love of the night-life, Max Baer was a likeable guy. When he trained at the Ace of Spades on the Kingston Bypass before the war, I found him a great character with a heart as big as himself. Considering at heart he wasn't cut out to be a fighter, in spite of his perfect physique and hitting powers, Maxie Baer goes down as one of the great characters of the ring. And he wasn't just a humorous glamour boy like some of the others—he was an outstanding heavyweight. He was a King who chose to be a Clown Prince!

CHAPTER VI

THE DARLIN' BYE

MAX BAER MAY have been the most successful of the fighting crackpots, but as a playboy he had nothing on Jack Doyle, a gossoon from County Cork . . . the character whom I christened the Darlin' Bye. Say what you like about him, but there was never a heavyweight born this side of the Atlantic Ocean who could pack in the fans like this Gorgeous Gael. He was the Handsome One alright . . . with a punch like a cannon-ball, a voice like a thrush, and, sure, wasn't he the babe the leprechauns visited before blarney was taken off the ration! Yes, my friends, Doyle had everything that goes to make a great fighter. Everything barring two essentials . . . a tough chin and the ability to fight!

I well recall his second meeting with Eddie Phillips at London's White City in the summer of 1939. Topping the bill was a match between Len Harvey and Jock McAvoy which was advertised as being for the world light-heavyweight championship. John Henry Lewis had arrived in London a few weeks earlier with every intention of defending his world crown against Harvey for a second time, but America's National Boxing Association declared the Negro's title to be vacant owing to the poor state of his eyes. The British Board doctors examined Lewis's eyes, and confirmed that in their opinion Lewis might risk blindness if he took further punishment in a fight. The Negro was not, therefore, allowed to box, and the Board then called in Jock McAvoy to meet Harvey, and decided that the winner would be recognised as new world champion.

Doyle could not even start to compare with either Harvey or

McAvoy as a pugilist, but the two miles traffic jam leading to White City Stadium was caused by only one man—and that was the Cork Stopper, who less than a year earlier with the same Eddie Phillips had knocked himself out flying over the ropes to be counted outside the ring without Phillips so much as landing a blow at this precise moment of the second round. Yet the British public still had faith in the colourful Irishman who had disappointed in nearly every big fight. The big crowd stampeded, and finally rushed from the cheaper to the more expensive seats. Harvey and McAvoy put up a great show, Len sneaking the decision with a grand-stand finish, although he was never seriously recognised as world champion once Billy Conn took over in America.

The cheers of the Harvey-McAvoy slam died as both boxers disappeared to their dressing rooms. Now the real excitement began . . . the entrance of the gladiators—or rather THE gladiator! All eyes were on Doyle. He thoroughly enjoyed every second of his long, long walk from his dressing room on to the track and down the gangway to the centre of the field where the ring was erected. I have a clear picture of him as I write. He was dressed in an all-white bath-robe. His dark curly hair was well groomed. He walked slowly and deliberately, the perfect showman as he paused for split seconds to acknowledge the adoration of beautiful women and the homage of complete strangers.

Phillips, a clever boxer and a pretty good puncher, but too highly strung for a pugilist, slipped into the ring almost unnoticed. He was the conqueror, but as usual he was tense and on edge. The Darlin' Bye entered the ring as sure of himself as any prima donna. He had everything mastered to a fine art . . . even the way he slipped off his robe. With exaggerated casualness he caused his biceps to swell like large grape-fruits, and expanded his chest to Tarzan measurements.

In his emerald green trunks he looked indeed a King of the ring . . . Hollywood fashion at least. Doyle was confident. He smiled patronisingly at Phillips, gave him a sarcastic "Best of luck, Eddie!", and then came out as the bell sounded throwing rights from every angle as though in a hurry to dispense with all this nonsense. Phillips slipped down, and Doyle now seemed the killer. He threw more rights, and Eddie looked about as comfortable as a diver who has just plunged into a bathing pool before it has been filled with water. Then it happened suddenly. The thing that could only happen to Jack Doyle. Phillips, boxing on the defensive, ducked his head as the Irishman rushed in, but instinctively, the Bow heavyweight stuck out a piston-like left which smacked the Irishman's delicate chin. Somebody ought to have shouted "Timber!" because the next second the Irishman was crashing backwards as stiff as an oak tree. The blow was more defensive than offensive but Doyle was down and out by a straight left! In fairness, to the Irish Thrush, the back of his head landed with a real thud on the canvas immediately in front of me. He lay like a warrior taking his rest!

Doyle's retreat to the dressing room was not so magnificent as his entrance to the ring a few minutes earlier. He bowed his head, and hurried back. I was not only the first reporter to see him afterwards, but the only one. Doyle really had had it, and the loser's dressing room is a lonely cubby-hole. Yet my heart warmed once more for this playboy who forced a grin and began to recite Kipling's "If" . . . "If you can face triumph and disaster, and treat those two impostors just the same," he muttered with a wry smile. Under the circumstances, I didn't put to words my thoughts of the moment and add . . . "Then you'll be a man, my son, but never a boxing champion!"

Doyle's first scrap with Phillips at Harringay had been even more sensational. It took place on a Tuesday evening in September, 1938, when we were all convinced that a fresh world war was about to begin. Hitler was at the peak of his military ravings, and none of us felt very secure about the future. I was the *Daily Express* boxing writer at the time. Lord Beaverbrook had an optimistic slogan which was appearing in the paper each morning . . . "There will be no war this year or next year."

There was less optimism in the building than in the newspaper. Sensible precautions had been taken, and on the walls were notices which read: "Follow the red arrow for A shelter." and "Follow the green arrow for B shelter." Furthermore, sandbags were being put on the roof, and a labourer was building an anti-blast wall between my desk and a window overlooking Shoe Lane.

I was due to meet John Macadam, the paper's columnist, at 6.30 before going to Harringay with him. Guy Eden, the Political correspondent, had just returned from Whitehall. "What's the bad news?" I asked. He was quite serious when he replied: "I think Britain will be at war with Germany before the week-end."

I joined Macadam in the little pub in Poppins Court which although it bears the name of the Red Lion, I have never yet heard it called anything other than "Poppins." We "celebrated" with a large Scotch before driving to Harringay for what looked like being the last big fight the pair of us would see in a long time as a much bigger fight was about to be promoted by Adolphus Schicklegruber.

The fight itself now seemed insignificant, but inside Harringay I banged into the promoter of the contest, the late Sydney Hulls, who was a good showman, a nice guy and a pal of mine. Syd was not in his usual gay mood. "Come and see your fine Irishman," he snapped. "The big so-and-so wants more cash than I agreed to pay him." Had he not looked so worried, I would have said Hulls was pulling my leg, but obviously something was wrong, and I went along with the promoter to the dressing room. There on the rubbing table covered in a green silk gown was Jack Doyle his arms folded across his chest as though he hadn't a care in the world. "What's the trouble, Jack?" I asked, and with that charm which comes from across the Irish Sea he smiled and replied: "Sure, but there's no trouble, Frankie me bye, but I'm glad to be seeing you. You're a pal of Syd and, I hope, of mine. So you're neutral. Now I'm going to ask you precisely the same question as I was putting to Sydney himself a few minutes earlier, and all I'm asking for is an honest and unbiased reply.

"Will you tell me now without prejudice who is that big crowd out there waiting to see . . . Eddie Phillips or Jack Dile?" The Blarney Boy had put me well and truly on the spot. Hulls was obviously in trouble, and I wanted to do all I could to help and not to hinder, but Doyle was asking a simple question, and the rascal knew there was only one answer, and I gave it.

"There, Sydney, me bye," said Doyle "you've heard the words from a neutral source, from a man whose word neither of us would doubt. What's a few pounds among friends?" Doyle was smiling as though he were wooing a Kerry Colleen, but he soon made it clear that if he didn't get what he wanted he intended putting on his clothes and walking out, leaving Hulls holding nearly ten thousand tough babies who would be hollering for their money back.

"You win, you Irish so-and-so," he hissed. Doyle insisted on having his purse money in advance. Hulls borrowed my fountain pen with which he wrote a cheque. What actual sum of money was on the cheque I did not see, but I did see the cheque handed to Doyle. Hulls told me it was for £1,000. I believe Doyle later insisted on and received a cash sum before he went in the ring. Tom Webster, the famous cartoonist, was called in to reason with him.

The fight was another Doyle fiasco. Nothing worth while happened in the first round. In the second, the Irishman made a lunge at Phillips, missed and, like the daring young man on the flying trapeze, sailed through the air with the greatest of ease, to land outside the ring. To this day, Doyle insists a certain gentleman rather friendly with Phillips rushed to help him up, but stood on his foot, and loosened his grip every time Doyle went to grasp his hand and heave himself up. Anyway, Jack was standing up by the Press seats when the timekeeper reached ten, and that was that! The Irish contortionist had knocked out himself without so much as landing a blow! It didn't stop him arriving at Hulls' bank next day and presenting his cheque for cashing.

It was several years later when I was playing golf with Syd Hulls that I asked him to tell me the sequel to the incident when I had loaned him my fountain pen to sign that cheque in Doyle's dressing room. What had once been a head-ache had now become laughable to Syd who explained: "I was in bed next morning, tired, angry and fed-up at what the Irish so-and-so had done to me at Harringay when the phone went. It was my bank, and I was told a Mr. Doyle was there when the doors had opened waiting to clear a large cheque. The bank wanted my O.K." Syd burst out laughing as he continued: " 'Stop it!' I growled, but Hetty, my wife, was in the room, and she intervened telling me that if in my business I stopped a cheque it would do me no good. So I took the wife's advice, and said 'O.K. pay it.' Anyway, an hour later Doyle was on his way to the docks to board the Empress of Canada to cross the Atlantic."

I had told you war seemed a certainty. But the day following the fight Mussolini intervened and suggested a meeting with Hitler, the British Prime Minister, Neville Chamberlain, and himself at Munich. Poor Mr. Chamberlain returned waving his umbrella and a bit of valueless paper signed by Hitler and Mussolini, and spoke of "Peace in our time!" True, the crisis passed for some months. This was sufficient for the Darlin' Bye to do some galavanting in America. He even took the Yanks by storm at first, but his inability to fight caught up with him quicker among the harder-boiled American fight fans. Doyle's ballyhoo went up in smoke in his third U.S. fight when he was beaten in one round by the huge Buddy Baer, kid brother of Max. The Americans didn't want to know anything after this. Not even the rendering of Mother Machree could save him!

But as usual Doyle enjoyed himself. He wedded an actress named Judy Allen, which brought the obvious wise-crack that Jack may have lost his punch, but he had found his Judy! Soon he was also to lose his Judy. She divorced him. He had a romance with Mrs. Delphine Dodge-Dodde, the automobile millionairess, after this, and then landed up South of the Border down Mexico Way with attractive Movita.

Doyle brought her to England. She sang nicely, but was always overshadowed by her colourful partner. When war came in September, 1939, Doyle and Movita were touring the music-halls and Doyle was still packing them in.

Later the Darlin' Bye was told he could either dig ditches or return to Eire. The Irishman still had his pride—in spite of his boxing record—and with his head held high he told a Civil Servant "The back of me hand to ye!" and off he went to the City where the girls are so pretty.

In Dublin he did manage to persuade the Irish to stage one fight for him against Chris Cole for the heavyweight champion-ship of Ireland. Again Doyle managed to end on his back in jig-time. He had several fights outside the ring and outside pubs, and the law-makers of his own country took him to task.

A couple of years back he turned up in London again—this time as a—razzler. And, to be sure, didn't the Darlin' Bye pack them in again at Harringay. I watched him make his début with sun-tan powder covering his legs, body and face, and a well-pulled up pair of trunks shielding a large chunk of middle-age spread. I saw quite a few razzlin' fiascos. He met again his old boxing foe, Eddie Phillips, under Atholl Oakeley's promotion, and this time Eddie was disqualified for PUNCHING Doyle, something one is not allowed in wrestling. Eddie should have known, in any case, that Doyle was never made to be punched!

I also saw a farce between Doyle and Two-Ton Tony Galento. Each had a fall, and then Doyle took some "terrible" blows to his side and it was announced he had retired with a badly damaged rib. But, believe me, Eve did far more harm to Adam than Two-Ton ever did to Doyle.

His last Harringay appearance was in the ring fully dressed. The crowd booed and hissed while the M.C. announced that Doyle had failed to pass the doctor.

Could Doyle have been a great fighter had he possessed a

steadier character? I don't think so—mainly because of that Dresden China chin. I must confess, however, that I was one of his earliest admirers when I first met him years before the war at the Star and Garter, Windsor, when he was a handsome young Irish Guardsman of eighteen. And if my admiration had gone, I still had a warm spot when he last called in to see me to practise a little more blarney on me after he had joined the Grunt and Groan Brigade.

At eighteen Doyle was certainly a striking figure. He caught little Old Mister Public's imagination in his first professional fight when he knocked out in one round a fair-head Barnsley heavyweight by name of Chris Goulding. The bout took place at the Crystal Palace.

It was the game but not too capable giant Jack Pettifer who first made it clear that the Irish Thrush couldn't take a punch. With straight lefts he had Doyle reeling and staggering in the first round of their bout. Only a wild rally by Jack saved the situation, and Pettifer was knocked out in the second round.

After this, a short little Frenchman, by name of Moise Boquillon, who weighed little more than a cruiserweight, nearly wrecked the Irishman's career at the Albert Hall. In the first round, Boquillon, crouching low, dropped Doyle every time he threw a right. The Irishman made another of his uncanny rallies, rushing out in the second round to knockout the Frenchman who completely changed his tactics and never seemed to attempt to land another punch.

The Darlin' Bye's British heavyweight championship fight with Jack Petersen at the White City in 1933 was yet another farce. Doyle had gone to France to sharpen up his defence under the eagle eye of Monsieur Descamps, shrewd little manager of Georges Carpentier, but it took more than an eagle eye to tie down the Gorgeous Gael. As usual he had a good time.

When he faced Petersen, he had a go for the first round, but landed one or two low punches for which he was warned. When the second round began he again threw more low punches, and after more warnings was disqualified to the disgust of the crowd, who were entitled to scream: "We wuz robbed!" Doyle himself became a sad man, because he never saw his £3,000 purse which was confiscated by the Boxing Board.

Doyle would like to have that money to-day, because although he earned thousands, he has kept little of it. If he had been born with more restraint, he might have earned £250,000. He retains his charm and blarney, but youth is not so easy to retain.

Doyle's failure to reach the top and stay there could be summed up in the words he once used in reference to himself. "Pretty Girls are made to love and kiss. Who am I to alter this?"

Of such philosophy are Casanovas made, but not heavyweight champions.

CHAPTER VII

THE MILLS BOMB

IT WAS A dismal night late in January, 1950, that the battered champion with the mop of gypsy-like hair sank to the canvas more weary than stunned by the left and right cross that had jolted his chin. The tongues of 18,000 British fight fans were paralysed and the exaggerated quietness was in keeping with a public execution. Perhaps they regarded it as such for the beaten champ had been one of their most gallant and beloved fighters. Now, as he half-tilted on to his haunches, shook his head and raised his glove to a bleeding mouth from which three teeth had been smashed from the gums, he looked too discouraged, too disheartened and too tired to beat the count. And in this position, Freddie Mills of the lion-heart, and once iron-jaw, surrendered the world's light-heavyweight crown in the last fight of his career to Joey Maxim of America.

Mills at 30 had done his best until he was knocked out in the tenth round. He had been out-manoeuvred, out-boxed and out-punched by the clever Italian-American from Cleveland, Ohio, whose real name is Guiseppe Antonio Berardinelli, but while there wasn't a British fan present who wanted to take the tiniest shred of glory from Maxim, everybody knew they had only seen the shell of Mills whose courage had won a warm corner in all their hearts. They realised Maxim was a punishing enough fighter, but that the last right which had smashed Freddie's teeth would not have brought the American victory against the old Mills. Nobody has ever accused Maxim of being a knockout specialist.

Perhaps they also knew, as I did, and as Freddie realised in his heart, he had never been the same man since the first

183

Lesnevich world title slam in May, 1946, when he had taken such a battering . . . even though he went on to win that supreme title from Lesnevich in a return fight two years later. They knew it wasn't the right fist of Maxim that had dethroned Mills, but a combination of punches starting from Lesnevich and continuing through Joe Baksi, Lloyd Marshall and Bruce Woodcock. The iron jaw had at last cracked. Mills had reached the end of the road and nobody had a clearer view of the situation than Freddie himself.

Some champions have faded from the hall of fame on such a dismal note. All their great deeds of strength and courage have been forgotten, but not so Freddie Mills. The fight fans loved him in the ring, and their affection is such that Freddie's popularity has grown rather than dimmed and he can still bring a boxing crowd to its feet if he walks into any arena. He achieved success inside the ropes because he had become the first Englishman to lift the world light-heavyweight title since old Ruby Bob Fitzsimmons had beaten George Gardner 'way back in 1903. But his success since taking a ringside seat on the outside looking in makes him a more remarkable character than the gladiator who performed inside the ropes.

To-day he is a wealthy young man. In addition, he is one of our leading promoters, and his personality and quick sense of humour have made him a "natural" in television, radio and film studio.

Remarkable for a fighter who early on had taken more punishment than most boxers, and who seemed in danger of ending punchy after those great slams with Lesnevich and Woodcock in the space of 21 days in 1946. He looked a sick fighter when one day he told me seriously he was considering packing up as a boxer. He complained of headaches and said he felt sluggish, but to his credit he came back to win a title and to prove himself one of pugilism's brightest boys outside, as well as inside, the ring; although I am still certain he lost something as a fighter after the pasting he took from Lesnevich at their first meeting.

Freddie Mills has never looked anything than what he is . . . a pugilist. His chest is deep-barrelled and hairy. He has a pug nose, a cauliflowered left ear—the souvenir of his booth-days and presented to him by that old warrior Gipsy Daniels who once knocked out Max Schmeling in one round. His jaw is square-cut. In fact, in appearance he might be some huge square of rock Epstein put his chisel to and named "The Pug."

Yet in spite of all this, Freddie would never have become a fighter had not fate bulldozed stubbornly through a maze of obstacles to put him on his path to fistic fame. Never was a world champion born in a less pugilistical setting than Freddie Mills. To start with, he was born at Bournemouth, an attractive resort on the coast of Hampshire. A town with a population of 145,000 citizens. A town that never in the long history of Britain had previously produced a boxing champion. And he was baptised Frederick Percival!

Bournemouth is not famous for anything so ugly as fighters. The town is proud of its luxury hotels, attractive gardens and fountains. Its warm breezes have long enticed the sick and aged with sufficient money to be wheeled in bath-chairs. It breeds angels, but few angels with dirty faces.

On top of this, Mills went to a school which completely ignored boxing. He did not take up the sport until he was 14, and possessed little natural skill. Even after he had won the world cruiserweight title in 1948, Mills was not a great boxer in the truest sense of the word. Yet something inside him— perhaps it was a knowledge of his great strength—urged him to wander from his family as a boy, seeking the tough boxing booths which toured the West of England, to earn a few shillings a day.

But he has no regrets that destiny tossed him into the fight game because the fists of this working-class boy pulled in £80,000. For thirteen fights in five years British promoter Jack Solomons paid Mills around £65,000—an all-time record earnings of a fighter in England.

Mills owes his start in the fight game to Jack Turner of

Bournemouth, a small-town promoter and boxing booth manager. Freddie's father, a marine dealer, who sold and bought scrap iron and steel, was not in the money. So Freddie quit school at fourteen to join a local dairy, earning a few shillings packing butter and rising soon after dawn each day to deliver the milk.

It was an elder brother, Charlie, who first roused the curiosity of Freddie for boxing. Charlie became a member of an amateur club. Freddie pleaded to be taken along one night and was won over at his first sitting.

Some evenings Charlie would teasingly spar up to his kid brother, who could not use a straight left and had not even an elementary idea of defence, but one night Freddie connected with a left swing completely staggering his taller and heavier brother.

Freddie could now think of little else outside of boxing. He had heard of Jack Turner, an ex-middleweight boxer, who was also manager of Albert Barton's travelling boxing booth.

So, skipping his milk round one day, Freddie cycled to Mr. Turner's home some miles out of Bournemouth. Turner's wife chuckled when the little snub-nosed boy said, "I've called to see Mr. Turner. I want to be a fighter."

It was Turner's idea to give the lad a sufficient lesson to cure him of his fistic ambitions, and to send him back home. The fifteen-year-old boy was taken into the gym, and Jack admits: "I knocked the kid about perhaps more than I should, but it was intended for Mills's own good. But to my surprise, the boy took all that was going, and kept coming back for more."

Turner realised Mills had something, even if only guts, and soon he was coaching Freddie at the gym. His next step was to enter young Mills in a novices' competition. Freddie took this in his stride, winning a poor-looking silver-coloured cup, but it was a start.

At sixteen he took part in his first professional contest, and was paid 18/6 for boxing a 6-round draw with George Haskett at Weymouth. Turner put him on at regular small-time shows, and so popular was the young local that the promoter began featuring him at the Westover Ice Rink in Bournemouth.

One night Freddie was matched with a veteran welterweight. Mills knocked his opponent out in the first round, but the veteran complained he had beaten the count. So Turner offered to re-match them the same night. One hour later the pair climbed back into the ring, and this time Mills hit his opponent so hard in the first round that there was never any question of his beating the count.

Jack Turner, being a promoter, was not allowed to hold a manager's licence, but he persuaded Freddie's father to sign a five year contract making Jack's brother, Bob Turner, sole manager.

To gain experience for Mills, Turner advised Freddie to join the booth. For twelve months young Mills toured the West of England, taking on all-comers and sometimes standing among the audience as a stooge to challenge his colleagues in the booth when no genuine challenges were forthcoming from the crowd. After this Turner and Mills joined the more famous boxing booth of Sam McKeown, and Freddie remained in McKeown's booth four seasons.

All this time Turner insisted that Mills should train and be coached in the mornings. At twenty he was regularly topping the bill at the Westover Ice Rink, and the better the opposition the better Mills fought.

In 1939 Britain went to war. Bob Turner joined the R.A.F., Jack Turner went to work on munitions in the Midlands, and Mills joined the R.A.F. In 1941 Mills flattened a useful Sheffield middleweight, Jack Powell, in one round while on service leave. Ted Broadribb saw Mills as a possible champion.

Broadribb, who had dropped out of the fistic limelight following his split with Tommy Farr after the Welshman's great battle against Joe Louis in 1937, approached Mills. It was found Freddie's five year contract with Bob Turner had only six weeks to go. So the Turners reluctantly sold out to Broadribb for £200.

Broadribb quickly brought Mills to London, and in his first

fight at the Albert Hall, Freddie knocked out Tommy Martin, the coloured heavyweight. Mills was in the big money for the first time.

He then picked up £375 for smacking down Tommy Reddington, and £750 for a one-round win over Jock McAvoy, the middleweight champion. In 1942 he collected £1,000 and became British light-heavyweight champion, knocking the shell of Len Harvey through the ropes and out in two rounds. Although this bout drew just over £12,000, Muldoon, the promoter, made a profit of only £200.

Mills was now big-time as far as British boxing was concerned, but he had arrived at a time when England was practically starved of good fighters. Because there were no light-heavyweights to challenge him—Mills never once defended the title he won from Harvey but relinquished his British and Empire crowns 8 years later when he retired after the Maxim fight—Freddie began to give away weight to the heavyweights.

The majority of British heavyweights were little better than the smaller fighters, and Mills flattened most of them with his smashing left swing, which was almost too wild to be classed as a left hook. Yet in 1944 he slipped up against Jack London, a veteran bald-headed heavyweight of Tony Galento build, and lost a points decision and the chance of wearing the British heavyweight crown.

In 1945 the R.A.F. shipped Sergeant Mills overseas to India, but when he came back in May, 1946, the war had ended and Britain was approaching the greatest boxing boom in its history.

Jack Solomons, previously a match-maker for the late Jack Cappell, had now taken over the role of Czar of British boxing. Mills had arrived in England only a few days when Solomons was offering him £6,250 to fight Gus Lesnevich for the world light-heavyweight title at Harringay, London, on May 14.

Mills, although not in shape, couldn't afford to let this opportunity pass, and grasped at the bank-roll. King Solomons ordered one of his biggest cigars, and announced his ringside seats would cost twenty guineas!

Within a few weeks Solomons had sold out. Not only had he collected a gate close on £50,000, but disappointed fans were offering to pay black-market prices to see the fight.

But it was not the old light-hearted Mills who came out fighting against Lesnevich. His snap was gone, and a sluggish Freddie for the first time showed apprehension. A year out of the ring had sapped his confidence. A couple of "warming up" fights would have been a wiser choice. He was not ready to tackle a world champion.

Lesnevich almost annihilated Mills in the second round. Four times Freddie smashed to the canvas for counts of 6, 9, 8 and 9. Only a fighter as tough as Mills could have survived such a hammering.

More remarkable was the fact that Mills the fighter came out for the third round, exploiting skill the like of which we believed he had no knowledge. He began to outbox Lesnevich with short left jabs, and by the fifth round the American champion looked a pitiful sight. His left eye was completely closed, blood dripped from his nose and mouth, and his legs were slowing down. And the reason is that Mills had a complete black-out from the second to the eighth rounds and was automatically following out the instructions his manager was shouting from his corner.

At the end of the ninth round it looked 100-1 on Mills as Lesnevich walked slowly and sadly to his corner, but fate had not yet destined that Freddie should overcome the enormous odds that were blocking his path to a world championship.

In the tenth round Mills came out carelessly and Lesnevich, still full of courage, gambled desperately and went in after this strong young fighter who was cutting him systematically.

The American brought over a crashing right hand which landed flush on Mills's chin. The English boxer stood for a split second like a statue. Lesnevich whipped over another right,

189

and Mills was down for 7. He rose in a dazed state and was sent crashing for 9. Gus, now a fighting fury, leaped across the ring and put Mills down once more. It was here that referee Eugene Henderson stopped the fight. Two seconds had been counted—and only four seconds remained before the gong would have sounded the end of the tenth round. Henderson was asked to appear before the Stewards of the British Boxing Board of Control to say why he had stopped the fight. The official was angry about this and resigned although he is again operating as "third man" in the ring.

The opinion of boxing officials was that the referee should have continued to count Mills, and was only entitled to stop the fight for the protection of Mills if the British boxer had risen and was not capable of defending himself. Certainly, Mills had not taken so much punishment in this round as he had in the second when the referee might have been justified in halting the fight. Controversy raged. Had the referee not stopped the fight the gong would have sounded after Mills had been down six seconds. Could Freddie have recovered sufficiently with sixty seconds' rest to beat the half-blinded Lesnevich? However, it must always be remembered that a referee doesn't know how many seconds of a round remain. Only the time-keeper knows that.

Three weeks later Mills climbed into the same ring for a gruelling twelve round non-title fight with Bruce Woodcock. Although Woodcock was awarded the decision—and rightly so, the heavyweight champion was cut to ribbons by the light-heavyweight champion.

But it was still not the old Mills. He complained of headaches and of sluggishness, and it was feared that while in India a germ had got into his bloodstream. He visited a Harley Street specialist for treatment, but on November 5, he was back in the Harringay ring for his battle with Joe Baksi.

This is one fight that should never have taken place, and I blame Manager Broadribb and Promoter Solomons for a bad match. Ironically, the fight took place on the night of Guy

Fawkes, and there was never any mistaking that Mills was taken for the Guy.

After his two punishing fights with Lesnevich and Woodcock here was a light-heavyweight giving away more than 28 pounds to one of the toughest heavyweights from America. To Mills's credit he landed two left swings to Baksi's jaw in the first round, and Baksi said afterwards: "One of those punches was the hardest I ever received in my life."

But afterwards was a massacre. Mills had too long played the role of "giant-killer." He could not really hurt Baksi who, by sheer weight and similar style of fighting, wore Mills down in six rounds.

For the first time in his career Mills surrendered after six rounds. Both eyes were bleeding, and he never had a chance in this one-sided match.

After this the Bournemouth fighter decided to stick to light-heavyweights. He was tired of being over-matched, and made his target the light-heavyweight crown. Soon he was knocking out Willie Quentenmeyer and Enrico Bertola, the Dutch and Italian champions.

Then came his fight with Lloyd Marshall, a coloured Cleveland veteran, at Harringay on a hot June night in 1947. This was to be the stepping stone to a return title fight with Lesnevich. Marshall was considered "washed-up" in America and looked a nice push-over for Freddie.

But Mills reached an all-time low. Never previously had he put up such a pathetic show, being knocked out in five rounds. He took the final count in a sitting position, looking down at the blood that dripped from his nose on to his glove, completely disinterested in the referee counting him out.

For the first, and only, time in his career Mills was booed from the ring. He left with his head hung low, and walked to his dressing room to apparent oblivion. The obstacles seemed too great for even fate to bring him that world title.

The verdict of an unbiased jury of 10,000 fight fans was that Mills was finished as a world title contender. That the punishing fights with Lesnevich, Woodcock and Baksi had taken their toll, and the only path left to Mills was the hard and crowded road of forgotten fighters.

But there was a story behind it. Mills was not fit and not happy. He had had words with Ted Broadribb. There were more words after the fight, and Mills threatened to quit the game that had brought him a fair-sized bank roll.

He had his Chinese Restaurant, and a mentally depressed Mills reckoned that Confucius in his wisdom could have advised on these lines: "Chop Suey. Him more profitable and less painful than chopped up champion."

"I am ashamed of my performance against Marshall" he told me the next day, "that I intend spending the next three months thinking over whether I should get out of the fight game before I'm a punch bag."

So Mills went into the country and tried to forget. Working on the Cambridgeshire farms, and at the blacksmith's forge owned by the father of Eric Boon, former British lightweight champion, he began to get back good health—physically and mentally—and in September, 1947, he appealed against the "death sentence" of the fight fans who witnessed the Marshall debacle by beginning his come-back.

Pol Goffaux (Belgium), Stephan Olek (France), Paco Bueno (Spain) and Ken Shaw (Scotland) were all accounted for, and so King Solomons began negotiations for the return title fight with Lesnevich at the White City Stadium, London, on July 26, 1948 . . . eve of London's Olympic Games.

Few in England gave Mills a chance, but he proved us wrong and gained revenge for the beating he had taken from Gus two years earlier. Twice in the eleventh round he dropped Lesnevich and all but knocked him out, before snatching the world title.

At last his destiny was fulfilled, and the boy who had not donned a glove or raised his fist at school was the new world champion.

But all Mills's worries were not over. Shortly after becoming champion he had a return of his headaches, and dizzy spells.

How Turpin failed to beat Bobo Olson. A faded Randy Turpin used bad tactics in his world middleweight title slam with Carl "Bobo" Olson at Madison Square Garden in October 1953. The British champion persisted in leaning on the ropes and became a target for Olson's two-handed attack. The American won on points to win the vacant world middleweight title.

"Last one up's a Cissy!" Max Baer wisecracks to the giant Carnera in their world heavy-weight championship fight, June 14, 1934, after they have tripped over each other. Baer stopped Carnera in 11 rounds.

He became so worried that he cancelled arrangements to meet Lesnevich for the third time at Newark, New Jersey.

With his manager and a Boxing Board official, Mills consulted the Harley Street specialist and hypnotist, Dr. A. P. Magonet. The report of this Canadian specialist was: "Subluxation (that is slight dislocation) of the vertebrae was suspected, and then confirmed by X-ray. After a series of manipulations the vertebrae were restored to their proper alignment and the symptoms disappeared, and the patient is fit to return to work."

Feeling happier, Mills accepted an attractive offer to fight the South African heavyweight champion, Johnny Ralph, at Johannesburg in preference to defending his newly won title against Lesnevich and in November, 1948, knocked out the inexperienced Ralph in 8 rounds in Johannesburg.

And so Freddie took things easier until the summer of 1949 when he made an unsuccessful bid to lift Bruce Woodcock's heavyweight title. This was the only bout Freddie had that year. He wanted rest, and also he found that every time he fought he had to tackle two opponents—one of his foes being the Inspector of Taxes. It just didn't pay him to fight frequently.

Mills was well beaten by Woodcock, and took the count in the 14th round. The deterioration, so clear in the Maxim fight seven months later, was already obvious and the blow that ended the meeting with Bruce would not have stopped the old Freddie Mills. He had once confessed to me that since the first Lesnevich fight a punch on a certain spot of the chin seemed to give him mental paralysis. Woodcock and Maxim found the spot.

Mills has come out of the fight game well. In many ways he has been fortunate because the light-heavy and heavyweight talent around in his early war-time career was almost nil, but good luck to him on the fortune he earned because of his courage and his desire to please the customers.

If you want to remember Mills as a great fighter, don't think of him as a heavyweight. He doesn't even rate as such, having made unsuccessful bids to win the title against Jack London and Bruce Woodcock. But in the eight years he held the British and Empire 12st. 7lbs. crowns there wasn't one British or Empire fighter around who was considered even good enough to challenge him, and so he relinquished both titles in 1950 without having once been called upon to defend them. What is more, he won the world championship. So he must go down as one of our greatest and toughest light-heavyweights.

When he was fighting, Freddie, with a twinkle in his eye, used to jokingly sing his own facetious words to the tune of "There's no bizness like show bizness." The Mills version went like this:

> "There's no bizness like the fight bizness,
> They smile when they're hit low:
> All the managers are such great schemers,
> 25 per cent is all they know.
> Managers go on for blinking ever,
> But where, oh where, do fighters go?
> There's no racket like their racket,
> Cigars are all the vogue.
> After every match they
> Come and take their whack,
> Into their cars to count their jack,
> While the poor old fighter
> Makes one more come-back
> On his bike he pedals for home.
> What a game this fight game has grown!"

Since his retirement, Mills has tried his hand as a manager and as a successful promoter, and bizness is good. There's no bizness like the fight bizness, Freddie, old boy!

CHAPTER VIII

". . . AND THE GOOD GIANT LIVED HAPPILY EVER AFTER"

THE CARNERA STORY reads more like a fable from the pen of Grimm or Andersen. If ever a living Gargantua stepped from fantasy into the realistic but sordid atmosphere of the blood, sweat, resin and sawdust of the prize ring it was Primo Carnera, the simple peasant of Sequals, Italy, who was to rise from the ignominy of a freak wrestler in a cheap French circus marquee to the status of adorning the world heavyweight boxing crown— the richest and most glamorous prize sport has to offer.

It does not make pretty reading, because never has the prize ring stooped to such callous and scandalous exploitation as in the rise, decline and fall of this Roman fistic Emperor, but like a fairy-story it has a happy ending. Because Carnera, tossed on the garbage heap in 1936 broke and semi-paralysed by those who had lived on his physical efforts and suffering in the ring, is to-day a wealthy man, thanks to his early knowledge of wrestling plus the miracle of television which swept America at the end of the last war. Commercial T.V. paid Carnera the Wrestler more dollars than Carnera the boxing champion had ever been allowed to glimpse by his army of percentage-takers.

Nobody takes professional all-in wrestling too seriously, but as an entertainment American T.V. viewers went for it in a big way after the war years. Only a few hundred would turn up at the venue itself, but millions watched it from their homes and in the bars of the United States. Without television, Carnera would to-day be something of a pathetic figure.

The Italian giant has been ridiculed as a freak who couldn't box, couldn't fight and couldn't punch. It has been said he was given a phoney build-up into winning the world heavyweight championship. Some of these allegations have been written by folk who never even saw him perform, but I still believe that Carnera, properly cared for, would have been an efficient if not a great world champion. His major weakness was his inability to take punishment on his lantern-like chin.

Big hitters like Max Baer, Joe Louis and a little-known Negro, Leroy Haynes, were later to expose this flaw in the giant's physical make-up. But to describe Carnera as a cardboard champion, who had neither ability, strength nor courage and a glandular buffoon who didn't know how to hold up his fists is both inaccurate and unfair.

The boys who, after—and I emphasise the word "after"—every big fight, tell you they knew it was a fake, declared Carnera's battle at the Albert Hall with Young Stribling, the handsome Georgia Peach, which ended in the disqualification of the American, was a set-up. How unfair and how wrong. I still remember being disturbed an hour after that bout on hearing the groans of Carnera as he lay stretched out on a table in a room which you could look down on from the press room of the Albert Hall. I pulled back the curtains, but quickly retreated as I saw the giant in obvious pain. He certainly wasn't acting.

I am not so naive as to believe his American handlers did not stage many of his early fights out there in such a way that there could be only one winner, but I do not believe, in spite of the cynics, that Jack Sharkey would have thrown away his world heavyweight crown. Remember, the world heavyweight title is worth a million dollars, so a million dollars must be found to bribe a fighter to throw away such a treasure. Carnera, as a boxer, was not, of course, a Jim Driscoll, but he had more skill than many heavyweight champions I have seen, and for a creature scaling above 19 stone he moved with surprising agility and daintiness. That he didn't punch his weight was obvious but nevertheless the Ambling Alp—as he was quickly dubbed by the late Damon Runyon—hit hard enough to flatten most heavyweights when he wanted.

I was thirteen when I first set eyes on Carnera, and I was at an age when the Italian giant made such an impression on me that I shall never forget him. It was in the autumn of 1929, and the late Jeff Dickson, that great Showman of Europe, brought him to London from Paris. The French-American boxing boss had begun to promote in this country, and had managed to secure the Albert Hall. Jeff's first big show featured Johnny Hill, the clever little British flyweight champion from Scotland, versus Frankie Genaro, of America, for the world title.

But a few days before the contest was due to take place, poor Johnny Hill collapsed in training and died later. Dickson did the next best thing by naming the popular Millwall fighter, Ernie Jarvis, as Hill's substitute, but as tickets had not sold too well even before Hill died, Dickson knew there could not now be a last-minute rush because, although Jarvis was a fine little scrapper, it was a fact that he had already lost to Johnny Hill.

So Dickson had a publicity brainwave and imported Carnera to fight Jack Stanley, a former policeman from Greenwich. I have said I was at an impressionable age. I can see him now as I stood gazing up at him for the first time in Dickson's office in Cecil Court off the Charing Cross Road. If I had been told he had arrived from Mars, I would have believed it, because never before had I seen such a sight. He was tall—6ft. 5¾ inches—but fairly well proportioned physically, and I found myself staring child-like at his huge head. His face was sallow and his teeth were like fangs, but although his lips were spongey and large, his big brown eyes lit up and the ferocious giant suddenly became a big friendly fellow.

The Man Mountain had shoulders almost as wide as two normal men. His legs were like trees; his feet enormous. Yet it was his ham-like fists and long fingers, as fat as beef sausages, that really made you gasp. At this time Carnera could not utter one word of English. He spoke from deep down in his throat, and his voice was as sweet as though he gargled with gravel. His favourite word sounded something like "Ugh!"

But he provided all the publicity Dickson wanted. Pictures soon appeared in most newspapers of him dwarfing City policemen, and wherever he walked he stopped the traffic. The night of the fight was a sell-out. Even the curiosity of the Prince of Wales had been aroused, and the Prince was at the ringside. The world title fight took second place. Everybody wanted to see this Roman giant who might have stepped from the twelfth to the twentieth century. Dickson had a complete sell-out for this, his first London venture, and he was only paying £100 all in for Carnera's services! The Italian was presented as only Dickson and his tiny French manager, Leon See, knew how. It was showmanship at its best. Monsieur See, a tiny man, had chosen pygmies as seconds to exaggerate Primo's size.

The crowd gasped at first and then laughed as Carnera entered the ring. They were given little value for their money, because Jack Stanley was down and out in less than two minutes, but they went away happy enough. Carnera had arrived as the eighth wonder of the fistic world. Dickson had become a successful London promoter at his first attempt.

Overnight the word Carnera became familiar. There wasn't a man, woman or child who didn't now know of his existence. He was in demand everywhere, and was immediately offered a stage contract and appeared first at the old Alhambra Theatre in Leicester Square on which site now stands the Odeon cinema. My father had managed to persuade Carnera to make a ring appearance at the Bermondsey Town Hall in aid of the local Catholic boxing club. To me fell the honour of going in a hired car to the Alhambra with an old friend, Charlie Darby, to escort the Big Fellow to Bermondsey.

We were taken to the side wings to watch the act. It was not brilliant, but the audience seemed satisfied. Carnera's weight was announced as 22 stone. His height was stepped up to 6ft. 8ins. He wore stage boots with false toes, which made his size 13 feet appear at least six inches longer than they really were. His sparring partners were announced as men all standing above six feet, whereas off-stage it was easy to judge the tallest was about 5ft. 8ins.

Primo shook me by the hand in the dressing-room, and laughed at the size of my small fist in his. He gave another great chuckle as he took off his boots with the false toes, and I noted he had now learned a few words of English—or should I say American—because to most questions he replied, "Okay!" His English lessons were taken every afternoon at the cinema where talkies had become the rage.

The journey to Bermondsey was uneventful apart from the fact that when Carnera attempted to put on the light in the back of the car he pulled the switch completely away in one huge hand—an action which brought yet another of those thunderous claps of laughter. Because my weight was then about eight stone and Charlie Darby scaled no more, the driver found the car cornering like a toboggan on ice, and the Ambling Alp was asked to sit dead centre in the back seat, and I moved forward to join the driver.

Carnera was a quick learner. He was still very much a novice when Dickson signed him for his second Albert Hall appearance against Young Stribling, the experienced American heavyweight, one month after the Stanley bout. I shall never forget this fight if I live to be as old as Methuselah.

Stribling, a handsome fighter, with a record of more than three hundred contests, was dwarfed by the Italian.

The Georgia Peach was a small heavyweight anyway, and weighed a little over thirteen stone which meant he was conceding six stone to his mountainous opponent.

Stribling, remarkably cool, took things easy for two rounds, poking out a light left, and staying away from his huge rival. But in the third round he decided the big novice was ripe for killing. William Lawrence let fly a right hand smack on Carnera's chin. It proved then and there that the Italian Alp's chin was nearer to china than granite, and could be cracked, because he was lifted off his feet and went down with a thud which all but caused the ring to collapse. But if it proved Carnera's chin was his big weakness, it also emphasised that poor old Da Preem had terrific courage and a much better fighting brain than most folk credited him.

I can see the collapsed and bemused giant rolling over. He recovered. At 6 he was on one knee, and with the coolness of an iceberg waved one huge glove, which looked like a brown pillow, to his corner to calm the hysterical Leon See, who was setting up a noise like a banshee. The gesture was crystal clear. It was as good as saying: "Don't panic, I'm okay."

Carnera was cool enough in those couple of seconds, but as he climbed off the canvas at 9 the whole fury within him was released. His dignity had been hurt. David had dared to topple Goliath. Carnera charged like a wounded boar at his small opponent. My young head wanted to burst with fear and excitement. Crack! A right hander put Stribling down, and such was the fury of the giant that he looked like going down to finish off the insolent little man who had dropped him. It was the only time in his career that Carnera was a terrifying monster. It was the only time he lost his temper in the ring.

The lightning action of Ted Broadribb, refereeing the bout, saved Stribling from serious harm. Broadribb grabbed Carnera's glove to steady him, and although the enraged giant nearly swung him away, the referee was able to restrain him sufficiently to begin the count over Stribling. The third round was nearly over, and the American survived, but when the fourth session began, Stribling quickly sank a low punch to Carnera's groin, and the would-be assassin was reduced to a shot bison writhing on the canvas in pain. Stribling, who some years later was killed while driving a motor-cycle in Georgia, admitted the blow was intentionally low. "Carnera that night was a wild animal," declared the Georgia Peach, "Nobody living could have conceded six stone and got away with it that night!"

It is difficult to excuse any fighter for punching deliberately low, but if any man can be excused it was Young Stribling. He was due for execution, and when danger is near we all might forget the Marquis of Queensberry Rules!

Broadribb was quick to see justice done when he disqualified the American. Those who cried "Fake" to this fight can have little knowledge of human emotions. It had been a bout of fury and passion. Stribling's action was one of self-preservation. The American could take a hard blow. He had faced some of America's best punchers. This fight disproved stories that Carnera couldn't hit. I endorse Stribling's belief that this night the enraged Carnera would have beaten almost any heavyweight in the world. But we never again saw him in such "killer" mood.

Dickson re-matched them in Paris nineteen nights later, and this proved a complete fiasco, the giant being disqualified for hitting his opponent after the bell had sounded the end of the seventh round. There wasn't any anger and passion in this unsatisfactory flop.

I saw Carnera again a few weeks later when he returned to the Albert Hall against a not very skilful German, Franz Diener, who was not even a match. I shall always believe that Carnera was never allowed to go all out again. After the first Stribling fight, Leon See, the only man who really knew his giant had a vulnerable chin, also realised that action might be taken to stop Carnera boxing if he harmed opponents. So the little Frenchman concentrated on showing his Roman how to box defensively. Day after day See insisted on practice in the gymnasium, and it was almost comical to watch Primo dancing round in the style of a flyweight poking out a straight left à la Driscoll. Wouldn't you laugh if you saw an elephant in a ballet?

It was after the Diener fight that the human battleship was launched. A course was set west across the Atlantic to New York and a dollar paradise. This move turned out to be the worst thing that could have happened. I doubt if any other human being since the dark middle ages has been treated so cruelly by a handful of dollar-hungry mobsters. Leon See, who I shall always believe had a genuine affection for his big and happy protégé, was the first to regret his move, because in a short time pressure was put on the little Frenchman to give up his interests in poor old Primo. The racketeers had moved into the fight game in a big way, and See, who at first resisted the offers of several partners who all wanted a piece of the Ambling Alp, was finally persuaded to sell out.

From then on it was Primo Incorporated! The poor fellow was no more than a huge carcass upon whom the vultures feasted. As far as they were concerned he didn't possess a soul, a heart, or any finer feelings. He was a whipping boy . . . a meal-ticket, and they couldn't feel the pain when that jaw, which Leon See knew must be protected, was eventually cracked by Max Baer, Joe Louis and Leroy Haynes. When he ended up in a New York hospital semi-paralysed in 1936 after being knocked out by Haynes his handlers did not visit him. In fact, one of the few visitors was Trevor Wignall, the famed *Daily Express* sports columnist, who knew him well in his early days in London, and who spent much time in trying to trace the forgotten giant.

When the Ambling Alp had first arrived in New York he had been given the ballyhoo as only the American fight boys can give it. His seconds were even more carefully chosen than they had been by Dickson for their lack of inches to make Primo stand up to his exaggerated description of a 6ft. 10 inches, 25-stone Colossus when he made his U.S. début against a hand-picked Swede named Big Boy Petersen, who had never embarrassed any worthwhile opponent. Petersen folded up like an obliging deck-chair inside the first round, and a barn-storming tour of the United States began.

Carnera was now being nursed along. The first big upset which the boys didn't bargain for was when the all-conquering giant was outpointed towards the end of 1930 by the light-hitting but clever veteran Jim Maloney of Boston in the Irishman's hometown.

Primo was shipped to Europe to let the laughs die down. In Barcelona he outpointed Paolino Uzcudun, the Basque

Woodchopper, and at the Albert Hall once more he took two rounds to stop Reggie Meen, our new heavyweight champion, in a match which should never have been allowed.

Back to America in March, 1931, he put things right outpointing Maloney in Miami, and then he had an easy tour until late that year he dropped another decision to Jack Sharkey. Another European tour followed for six months in 1932, when he had easy victories in Paris, Berlin, Milan and London. I saw him stop George Cook—another ridiculous match—because poor old George, who had been stopped in two rounds by the Italian in America, could hardly reach the giant to hit him in the navel. This fiasco lasted four rounds, and Lord Lonsdale protested that he didn't want to see another such travesty of a contest.

It was in May, 1932, that Carnera was beaten for the only time in England—by the coloured Canadian, Larry Gains. The fight took place at London's White City, and there was the usual Dickson ballyhoo. Both boxers wore white gloves, and Carnera, boxing defensively, was outpointed over 10 rounds by the clever Canadian.

It was a dull bout with little interest until the last two rounds when Gains, realising Carnera wasn't able to hurt him, moved in with great speed and aggression and came close to putting the Italian down as he cracked right after right on the giant's jaw. Had the bout been over 12 or 15 rounds, I believe Gains would have beaten Baer to the task of knocking out the Alp.

Once again Carnera returned to the States where, after another careful build-up, he finally won the world heavyweight crown in the summer of 1933, knocking out Jack Sharkey with a right uppercut in the sixth round. In his previous contest, he had been involved in a tragedy when Ernie Schaaf, a friend of Sharkey, had died in a New York hospital after being beaten in thirteen rounds. Ever since that night in 1929 when I felt my heart bursting with apprehensive excitement as the enraged giant felled Stribling I had believed Carnera would one day kill an opponent.

His critics who derided him and said he couldn't punch his way out of a paper bag insisted Schaaf's death was due to earlier injuries received in a ten-rounder with Max Baer six months before. Baer, admittedly, was a murderous puncher, but although Carnera could not hit like Baer, Louis, Schmeling or Rocky Marciano, whom I rate in the Baer class, he could hit sufficiently to be feared.

The Carnera bubble was really exploded nine months after he won the title from Sharkey when he defended the crown against Tommy Loughran, the former light-heavyweight champion, who was noted for his skill but was regarded as a powder-puff puncher. Although six stone lighter, Tommy made Carnera look silly, and took him the full fifteen rounds. The Italian was booed that night for continually treading on Loughran's feet!

In June, 1934—a year after he had won the crown—the Ambling Alp was smashed to smithereens by Maxie Baer. Baer put Carnera down three times in the first round and then, in between much frowning, scowling and jeering, severed the giant's mouth, split his brows, and reduced him to pulp in 11 rounds. The irony of this was that Baer confessed that he really discovered Carnera's weaknesses while sparring with him in a Hollywood film, "The Prize-Fighter and the Lady" in which Baer starred and Carnera was a well-paid stooge to appear with him in a world heavyweight championship shot in the film.

Yet still they tried to bring him back. Poor Primo knocked out some bums in South America in 1935, but was falling to pieces fight by fight, and then they gave him an up-and-coming Negro from Detroit who was the talk of the fight game. This young coloured boy shattered Carnera in six rounds in Madison Square Garden. His name was Joe Louis.

Carnera came back sufficiently to stop Walter Neusel in four rounds, but that was his last worthwhile triumph. His followers, realising his days as a meal-ticket were over, disbanded Primo Incorporated, and threw him in with Leroy Haynes for a pay-off. Haynes flattened him in three rounds in Philadelphia on March 16, 1936, but because they didn't believe the "unknown"

Haynes could really do that to *them*, they tossed the shell of Carnera back into a Brooklyn ring eleven days later. This time the Negro took nine rounds to smash and batter Carnera to pulp, so that he was carried by six men from the ring, battered, bleeding and paralysed, and later taken to a hospital to lie alone for days. An indelible disgrace to a sport even as callous as boxing.

Primo was eventually shipped home to Italy on a stretcher, and back amid the peace of the little town of Sequals he began to nurse back to health, but foolishly fought in Paris and Budapest in 1937, being twice beaten.

During the war, there were the usual inaccurate reports of his being wounded, executed, and captured . . . just as Max Schmeling and Paolino Uzcudun had also been wrongly reported as killed or missing. All we know for sure is that the big simple fellow joined the Italian Sniper Brigade to help the Allies in 1943 and that in 1946 he had one more fight, but lost to a fighter I had never heard of before, Luigi Musina. As soon as he was able, Carnera returned to America—scene of his dreadful exploitation sixteen years earlier.

But this time there wasn't any Carnera Incorporated. Just a one-man-band . . . a wrestler without six or seven hangers-on taking chunks off his income. Soon he was to become the No.1 wrestler in America as far as the box-office was concerned. I am not fond of all-in razzlin' because it is many years since I ceased to believe Father Christmas came down the chimney or that the stork brought the new baby, but I am glad that such a sport exists if only to give a second chance to the first son of an Italian mosaic-cutter from Sequals whose glands functioned so abnormally that he became like a creature born centuries out of his time. To-day Primo is a dollar millionaire, has an estate in California and a nice family. So I for one do believe in fairy stories ". . . and the good giant and his princess lived happily ever after."

CHAPTER IX

BENNY BEAT THEM ALL . . . ALL EXCEPT
JOHN BARLEYCORN

SOME OF THE most outstanding flyweights who have carried the
Union Jack to the highest pinnacle of international pugilism
have come out of Scotland. The land of the heather has given
us Tancy Lee, Elky Clark, Johnny Hill, Benny Lynch and Jackie
Paterson . . . champions all, but the greatest was Lynch.
Poor misguided Benny! Invincible against any living flyweight
the world could pit against him, yet defenceless against himself
. . . himself and John Barleycorn.

If ever a champion committed professional hari-kari it was
the wee Scot who, with the world at his feet, tossed away a
golden crown and tumbled off his throne into . . . yes, I'm
afraid it is true . . . the gutter.

I have seen scores of champions ride the dizzy heights
oblivious that they can't abuse Nature forever. Eventually the
pay-off has struck like a thief at night, and next morning their
world has crumbled, leaving them to totter along the already
over-crowded cobbles of Dead-End Alley.

There have been many tragedies of the ring, but the sudden
decline and fall of Lynch surpasses any other boxing drama
because the Scot turned his back on fame, fortune, a world
crown, good health and self-respect when only 25 and at the
peak of his career.

To-day Lynch should be among us . . . a living memorial
of the supreme sporting stock produced by Britain. He should
be a wealthy and respected citizen. Instead, poor Benny Lynch,
once a pocket-Hercules, died in a Glasgow tenement at 33
having lost everything.

I do not wish to dwell too long on the failure and the human weaknesses of the little Scot of whom I was very fond. I would prefer to tell you more about his greatness, his fairness inside the ropes, his ability to box like a wizard and to punch with the power of a featherweight. Above all, it must be remembered this little man who can no longer defend himself against the many charges that have been written against him did little harm to anybody apart from himself. He was his own worst enemy, but I doubt if he had many foes in this world. Had he been born in a different environment, and possessed stronger will-power with which to protect himself from the bad influences of some early acquaintances I might now be writing a different story.

Lynch and Jimmy Wilde were the two best flyweights the world produced. The little Welshman was more amazing because, weighing around 6st. 10lbs., he knocked out opponents sometimes nearly two stone heavier. But would he have been able to give away over a stone to the tough Scot with the wicked right hand punch when both were at their best? This is a question that can never be answered, and a question to which I would not like to have to supply the correct result.

The magnificence of Benny Lynch could only be appreciated when he was fighting for a title. On those occasions he trained religiously, but in some of his non-title bouts he was a shadow of himself for the simple reason that he was often far from fit. Lynch dropped two decisions in overweight matches to Jimmy Warnock, the Belfast southpaw. I don't wish to take any credit from the Irishman who was a grand fighter, but I could not see him beating the Lynch who knocked out Jackie Brown and Peter Kane in title bouts, and who gave as immaculate an exhibition of boxing as has been seen when he outpointed the Filipino, Small Montana, over 15 rounds at Wembley in the fastest flyweight contest I ever saw.

Those three bouts showed us the Scot at his best. Against Brown at Manchester in 1935, he was a compact destroyer. The Manchester boxer, who had won the world title from the

Frenchman, Young Perez, three years earlier, was noted for his speed. For a boxer who moved so quickly Brown punched exceedingly well. A few months earlier Lynch had held him to a draw in a 12-rounds non-title contest, but Brown didn't know what had hit him in the affair at Manchester. The massive-shouldered little Scot released terrible blows and Brown was shattered in two rounds.

His victory over the American champion Small Montana in 1937 satisfied Americans that Lynch was undisputed world champion. The brown-skinned Montana was a smooth boxer. He didn't carry a big punch but had a wonderful defence. The critics were unanimous that to win, the Scot would have to bring over one of his Sunday punches in an early round. Otherwise, they declared, Lynch would never catch up with Montana who would proceed to give him a lesson in speed and science.

So Lynch put on a show of skill that left ringsiders gasping. Every trick Montana revealed was trumped by the Scot. The faster the Filipino set the pace, the more magnificent was Lynch. For 15 rounds the customers were entertained to one of the most classical and entertaining championship fights it has been my pleasure to watch.

Montana was never disgraced, but Lynch, usually a flat-footed block-buster, this night was the dancing master, the professor of all the arts of self-defence, and at the end, when his right glove was held high in victory, ringsiders stood, clapped and cheered for minutes, carried away like entranced music lovers at a Prom concert.

Nine months later Lynch featured in yet another flyweight epic when he battered Peter Kane, the Golborne blacksmith, to defeat in thirteen rounds at Shawfield Park, Glasgow. This was not a classic like the Montana fistic-symphony, but a thrilling and punishing battle showing Lynch again in the role of a terrible ring-slayer. Any Scottish fight fan will tell you this was the greatest flyweight slam in history.

Glasgow certainly was fight-crazy that night. Thousands of

men, women and children lined the streets to watch the crowds pass on their way to the football ground. Between 40,000 and 50,000 fans tried to get into Shawfield Park at the same time. There was such congestion outside the main gates that it didn't matter whether or not you had a ticket. You couldn't get inside. Thousands didn't see the fight. On top of this, the heavens opened and it poured all night. But the crowd inside didn't notice the rain as they watched the most destructive pair of flyweights since the days of Jimmy Wilde tear into each other like wild-cats. Never have two such punchers of eight stone clashed in the same ring together.

Kane was a raw youngster of 19 with a terrific punch, but little defence. He had plenty of colour, and danced around the ring at great speed always moving in on his opponent, staring at him with those large Eddie Cantor-like eyes. Up to now he was undefeated and believed he could lick anything in the world at 8 stone.

Lynch, the better boxer and slightly the stronger puncher, was mature and experienced. This was proved in the first seconds. Kane, as usual, came bouncing out of his corner with the enthusiasm of a puppy. Lynch, tucking his chin behind his powerful left shoulder, moved in more cautiously, but as Kane met him, Benny hooked to the body and then struck immediately with a right cross to Peter's chin. Some 33,000 rain-soaked spectators who had managed to squeeze their way into the stadium gasped as the young challenger went into a sitting position. The surprised look on Kane's face told its own story, and so did his action in rising at the count of 3. An experienced fighter would have taken another five seconds before going into battle again.

For 13 rounds, Kane punched away, as game as any fighter who had stepped into any ring, but he revealed after the bout was all over that he didn't remember anything after that first right had smashed against his chin. For a man suffering from a mental black-out, Peter put up a remarkable performance and, although out-generalled, caused some anxious moments for Glasgow fight fans and for the men in Lynch's corner.

Even in the second round he let go a number of hammer-like right-handers on the Scot's chin, and although Lynch wasn't in danger of being knocked out, he was shaken. Kane kept on moving in round after round fighting instinctively, trying to smack down the calculating slayer facing him. All the time, Lynch remained cool. The difference between the two men was that, whereas the Golborne battler's punches were often wild, Benny seldom wasted a blow.

By the twelfth round the patient Lynch could see Kane was just about "all in" and so the Scot rushed from his corner and battered the blacksmith against the ropes, so that Peter was reeling drunkenly although still refusing to go down, but the human body cannot always hold up a game heart for ever, and a left hook dropped Peter for 3. He rose and chased after Lynch still by instinct as blood poured from cut lips and nose. The bell saved him . . . for one more round at least.

The thirteenth was to be the end. Kane waded—or rather staggered—towards the champion. Lynch steadied himself before releasing a left hook which dropped the Lancashire boy in a heap. He was up at 7, but incapable of defending himself, and so the Scot took careful aim, and a smashing cross to the chin sent Peter crashing to remain lying across the bottom strand of the ropes, out to the world. A grand little battler had been annihilated by a superb champion.

Lynch was never the same fighter again. He was drinking heavily, and didn't seem to care that he was the most out-standing flyweight in the world. Five months later he boxed Kane in a non-title fight, and Peter shared the decision.

I travelled to Glasgow to see him defend his title against the American champion Jackie Jurich of California. Benny hadn't trained. There was a gasp at the weigh-in when it was announced he was 6½lbs. overweight. Poker-faced Lynch showed no emotion, although he knew he had lost his world crown on the scales.

The fight went on at catch-weights, and Lynch, in spite of his lack of condition, chopped down Jurich in 12 rounds. In another three months Benny had deteriorated still more and lost to Kayo Morgan over 12 rounds at Glasgow.

One more month saw him reach the depths in his last fight—the tragic affair against Aurel Toma, a fair bantamweight from Rumania, who would have been easy prey for the Lynch who had knocked out Kane only 12 months earlier.

This was the most tragic fight I ever watched. Benny had gone completely round the bend of the road. He was bloated and far from fit and what is more he had been drinking. I called to see him in his dressing room before the fight. He had lost every bit of self-respect as a fighter.

As a contest it turned out to be a farce . . . or rather a tragedy. Benny stumbled round the ring incapable of throwing a serious punch, and an open target for the little Rumanian who, as a fighter, was not fit to wipe the boxing boots of the Lynch we had known some six months earlier.

Efforts were made to save Benny from himself, but he was beyond rescue. He never looked forward again. All that remained was a wonderful past, a shameful present, and no future. He died still a young man in Glasgow in 1946.

Four other Scottish flyweights besides Lynch won the British flyweight title. *Tancy Lee* caused a sensation when at 33 and a father of six children he took the championship off Jimmy Wilde. *Johnny Hill*, who died when training for a world title slam with Frankie Genaro; *Elky Clark*, who lost a world title decision on points to Fidel La Barba at Madison Square Garden in 1927—Elky retired after losing the sight of his right eye to become a boxing writer in Glasgow; and, lastly, but not least, *Jackie Paterson*, the Glasgow "southpaw" who not only won the British, Empire, European and World flyweight titles, but also the British and European bantamweight championships.

Paterson, for my money, was the outstanding Scottish fighter next to Benny Lynch. Although he was a "southpaw" he did what no other Scottish fighter did—won six professional titles including the world flyweight crown. Jackie was a grand puncher—the next best to Lynch.

He was born at Springfield, Ayrshire, in 1920, a son of a coal miner, but was taken to America when he was four, and remained there twelve years. Yet when he returned to Glasgow he had not lost his Scottish accent. Back in Glasgow he joined the well-known Anderston club, and took part in the Scottish A.B.A. championships.

He did not win an A.B.A. title and turned professional early in 1938. Immediately his left hook began knocking over the best flyweights in the country.

Within sixteen months of turning professional he had won the vacant British flyweight title knocking out Paddy Ryan. The vacant Empire title was added six months later when he beat Kid Tanner.

In 1943, Jackie won the world flyweight crown knocking out Peter Kane in 61 seconds. He later won the European bantam title on a foul from the Frenchman, Theo Medina, and in 1947 took the British 8st. 6lbs. crown off the fading Johnny King.

I always felt Jackie had great difficulty in making 8 stone. Sometimes he ducked under the ropes looking drawn—particularly the night he lost his world flyweight crown to Rinty Monaghan in Belfast in March 1948, when the Irishman knocked him out in 7 rounds. Paterson, I should say, was beaten before he came into the ring. His legs were shaky, and it wasn't the power of Rinty's punch so much as Jackie's own weakness that licked him.

Paterson married a grand girl in Helen, and they have two splendid boys in Jackie and David. Helen has always been a big help to Jackie, and has a shrewd business head. Jackie himself always seemed pretty smart, and used to tell me he intended earning all he could from the fight game as quickly as possible in order to get out while at the top, I believed he was one pugilist who was really smart.

Unfortunately, the betting bug bit him, and bit him badly.

Helen couldn't influence him. As the holder of six titles he was able to command big purses and he earned nearly £35,000 before dog-racing began to get a grip on him.

I was in Glasgow one day for a Scotland v. England soccer international at Hampden Park. I had tea at their home. Jackie was breaking his neck to get off to the dogs. Little did I realise that in four years he would have lost everything and was to eventually land in the bankruptcy court.

Jackie, having lost so much money to the bookies, decided to switch and become a bookmaker, but it didn't work out. Many of his friends were quick to collect their winnings, but slow to pay what they owed, and Paterson was forced to close down.

Jackie went to America with the idea of settling down, but that didn't work out either and he returned to Scotland.

The last I heard of him, he was earning a small wage doing a simple job in Scotland. I am glad to record Jackie and Helen were happy.

Although Jackie threw away a fortune, he still has the love and affection of a wife and family who still regard him as the Champ. Is such a guy really poor?

CHAPTER X

KING OF FISHTICUFFS

On DECEMBER 10, 1900, there was unusual excitement over the birth of a boy to humble Jewish parents who sold fish in Middlesex Street, the romantic junk street in London's East End known as Petticoat Lane. A tough, notorious highway of stalls and barrows in which you can purchase anything from a pair of kippers off the honest trader to the diamond from the odd characters who patiently lounge around waiting for the right customer.

Petticoat Lane has always been an exciting showplace as well as a bargain market for the women of the East End. It is an incongruous alley of hard-working and legitimate traders plus the smart operator who grows fat on the philosophy that a sucker is born every minute of the day. So you have the choice of picking up a bargain you couldn't buy for love nor money at the more luxurious stores in the West End. Or you may buy back the gold watch so skilfully lifted from your person at the racetrack two days earlier.

Ordinarily, the birth of a baby in Petticoat Lane's thickly populated flats is no more important an event than taking out a license for a dog. But on that December morning, Petticoat Lane was talking about the baby boy with five fingers as well as one thumb on each hand that the stork had dropped at the home of Solomons, the fishmonger, and his wife.

Some neighbours giggled. Some whispered it was an omen of bad luck. The poor mother nearly passed out believing she had delivered a freak into an already troubled world. The amily doctor was more interested than concerned. The two extra fingers were perfect. But at the request of the distressed

Mrs. Solomons he arranged for the fifth fingers to be removed from each hand soon after birth.

So Jack Solomons, the fishmonger who has become Britain's greatest fightmonger, was born with the advantage of two extra fingers with which to grasp the fortune he has accumulated from fish, fights, and horse and dog gamblers. In 1945 I referred to him as Mister Boxing, King Solomons and King Cod. Since that date he has made such strides that he now rivals Tex Rickard and Mike Jacobs for the honour of the title of the greatest promoter in history. Had he been born in New York instead of London he may well have outstripped both Tex and Mike. Tex had Dempsey as the magnet for the million-dollar gates. And Mike seldom moved without Joe Louis. The Brown Bomber was tied closer to Jacobs than a skin graft. Had Solomons been able to handcuff the two greatest heavyweights of the last thirty years he would have been unchallenged as the world's greatest showman.

As it is, Solomons himself believes in monopoly and has British—and European—boxing sewn up pretty tightly to-day. I am against this on principle, but am forced to admit that the tactics of Rickard, Jacobs and Solomons to absorb and almost control the sport is the only recipe for complete success in the fight game. Promoters who are not able to tie-up the champions remain small-time.

Solomons is not in boxing for his health—any more than was Rickard, and Mike Jacobs, or is Mike's successor, Jim Norris of New York's International Boxing Club. But Solomons gets more laughs out of the fight racket than most big promoters. He is a fat jolly fellow who quickly makes friends in every part of the globe because he is always smiling—even when a cloud bursts the day before an open-air show or when the champion phones to say he's broken a bone in his hand and the fight's off.

Solomons loves the limelight. Hates to be alone, and always has round him a crowd of his East End buddies, relics of the days when he himself was small-time. Has a passion for champagne and oysters, but above all enjoys his ten-inch cigars.

Since he smokes six a day—that's sixty inches of tobacco—he is seldom seen without one of his gigantic Havanas, which cost him £1,500 each year.

He can't resist picking up a telephone to call a friend—even if only to shout, "Hi, there, Sonny Boy! Just called to make sure you didn't die in the night." Spends an hour each day in the hairdressing saloon. "I think out my best plans when I'm being shaved—especially when dealing with the cut-throat boys!"

Until recently Solomons could be found at his East End fishmonger's shop in Ridley Road every morning between 7 and 10. Twice a week he was buying fish at Billingsgate at 6 a.m. To-day he leaves the shop in charge of his brother Maxie, but still visits Ridley Road weekly to make sure the customers are being satisfied.

At midday he will be found in his boxing office and gymnasium in Gt. Windmill Street, a stone's throw from Piccadilly where his office overlooks the Windmill Theatre. In the afternoon he spends a couple of hours at his Mayfair bookmaking office.

At night Solomon's work continues. He dines in the West End, entertaining friends from America and all parts of Europe. His wife seldom sees him and says the day Jack quits the fight game for good she'll be happy. But England's Mister Boxing could no more quit the fight game than he could give up cigars.

Don't underestimate the Wisdom of Solomons. He is no fool. Already he has become the only true international boxing promoter, having invaded Paris, Stockholm, Dublin, Melbourne and Johannesburg as well as every big city in Britain prepared to empty its pockets to Jolly Jack.

His success has been such that he has made such showmen as Charles B. Cochran, Arnold Wilson, Harry Jacobs, Jeff Dickson and Sydney Hulls appear small-fry in their attempts to put over boxing in England.

Since 1946 Solomons has paid £200,000 to American fighters who were tempted to sail or fly the Atlantic. If proof was

216

needed that the U.S. promoters had to watch every move made by Solomons I refer to the boast of Sol Strauss and Harry Markson in 1948 that Gus Lesnevich would never defend his world's light-heavyweight crown against Freddie Mills in England.

Solomons arrived in New York apparently only interested in the Joe Louis-Jersey Joe Walcott heavyweight championship at Yankee Stadium. The Twentieth Century Sporting Club ignored him. One day, in fact, Mike Jacobs, who might be excused because of ill health, rattled his dentures at Solomons in the offices of the Twentieth Century and snapped, "Get the hell outa here."

Solomons "got." But he went with something Mike wanted badly, and that something was Lesnevich, required by the Jacobs organisation for a Louis bout in September. Bad weather caused the Louis-Walcott fight to be postponed for two nights. So Solomons sailed to England with Lesnevich and his manager, Joe Vella, and didn't bother to wait for the big fight. He had accomplished what he really came for, to outbid Jacobs for Lesnevich and to make doubly sure by personally escorting Gus to England. He had to talk in terms of £17,500, but he won, and with Lesnevich leaving his title in England in the care of Mills it was adding insult to injury to Jacobs, who never previously had to face up to serious financial competition from an English promoter. Later Solomons made the power of his bank balance felt when he secured Lee Savold for the London fight with Bruce Woodcock.

Solomons, unlike Jacobs, has had no Joe Louis to tie up for the rest of his fighting life. He has risen to the top in Britain, often playing around with names that were not even top-class. He put over glamourised boxing in such a way that the fans were falling over themselves after the way to pay £21 for ringside seats. As a kid, Solomons roughed the way of all the kids born in Petticoat Lane. At twelve he was pushing a heavy barrow load of fish at five o'clock each morning from Billingsgate to his dad's fish stall in the Lane. But he was crazy about the fight game and entered it the hard way. At sixteen he won his first professional fight, boxing under the name of Harry Crossman, knocking out a lad named Ted Green in two rounds. He was paid 16/6 for his work.

He was on top of his own little world of fish and fights, and dreamed of fame and fortune as the Champ. At seventeen, still using the name of Crossman, he beat Harry Berry in 4 rounds. At eighteen he was too ambitious and, this time using the name of Kid Mears, took on a classy boy named Young Joe Brooks who, incidentally, was Jack's brother-in-law, at Southampton. Solomons was paid £7 10s. and in five rounds was knocked colder than one of the cods on his barrow. He spent the £7 10s. on a present for his girl friend, Fay, who was heart-broken at the rough way her Jack had been handled, declared the present was bought with blood-money and warned him that he would have to decide between love and fighting. He chose Cupid, and after all these happy years of married life Jack tells you to-day: "Fay was dead right. I would have had my brains knocked out."

Although Solomons kept his word, never again boxing anything more dangerous than kippers, he could not stay out of the fight game. At thirty-one he staged his first promotion in the East End, boasting to Billingsgate, "I'm gonna knock the East End cold." Mister Greenhorn lost £300. But Solomons did not weep at the sight of empty saddles in the old corral. He burst out laughing at his own folly, and this gift of being a good loser is one of the secrets of his popularity.

A year later he took over a derelict church in Devonshire Street in the East End and renamed it "The Devonshire Club" after the high-class West End club. He charged only half-a-crown on Sunday afternoons. On Friday evenings his ringside was a bob and the gallery sevenpence.

Soon the Devonshire Club became the nursery of British boxing. Boys from all over England arrived, hitch-hiking from the North of England. In this smoky little former church where from 1,500 to 1,800 fans were packed in like sardines twice a

218

week, Solomons developed a string of British champions—
Kid Berg, Dave Finn, Johnny Softley, Harry Lazar, Tommy
Hyams, Jim Brady and Eric Boon.

Pedro Montanez received £12 10s. from Solomons for
fighting in the Devonshire Club. In the same year he fought in
Madison Square Garden for the world title!

Yet Solomons was still only an East End promoter. In the
West End he did not count. And then one day in 1935 a
fourteen-year-old blacksmith's son from Chatteris, a small
village in the Fen district, arrived on a bicycle. Solomons
chuckled at the size of the stocky youngster, who said that his
name was Boon and that he could punch harder than anybody
of his own weight. Boon forced a draw with Young Higgins.
Soon he was a sensation in the East End. Solomons became his
manager and for three years he had only to put on Boon and
the Devonshire Club was sold out within a matter of hours.

Soon there was nobody left to fight Boy Boon except the
champion and Solomons moved in on the West End when, at
eighteen, Boon was matched for the lightweight title with Dave
Crowley at Harringay late in 1938. Crowley was knocked out,
whereupon Syd Hulls, Britain's big promoter at that time,
signed Boon for a series of fights. It was, strictly speaking, a
verbal "contract" because, although Hulls had exclusive rights
of Boon, there was never anything in writing at any time,
although both Hulls and Solomons honoured all their
agreements.

In the summer of 1939 Hulls, Solomons and Boon crossed the
Atlantic—cabin class. Solomons was still very much the
successful East Ender, not sure of himself in the West End—
a Mister Nobody in New York—but he was learning quickly
from Hulls the tricks of the trade of big-time promoting.

He promoted his first championship fight in July, 1945,
between Bruce Woodcock and the bald-headed British heavyweight champion, Jack London, on the Tottenham Football
Ground in London. Solomons had to guarantee £7,000 before
the day of the fight for entertainment tax and the boxers' bond

money. In all, he stood to lose £10,000 if the fight flopped. But the sun shone brightly and he cleared for himself £400. Although he took in £25,000—£12,000 went in tax alone. But with Woodcock winning the title in impressive manner, Solomons had arrived for the first time as Britain's Mister Boxing.

He has not looked back since. After staging the successful London-Woodcock championship which was to bring him a five year tie-up with Bruce at great profit to both, his next ambition was to stage a world title fight in Britain. He did this in September, 1946, persuading Ike Williams, the coloured world lightweight champion, to defend his crown against Ronnie James on the Cardiff City soccer ground.

I knew by this time that Solomons was more than a good promoter. He was a born showman. He made the crop of would-be successful promoters, who had come on the scene during the war, appear like fistic pygmies, and he had something more than Jeff Dickson and Sydney Hulls who were pretty good promoters. All he needed now was a fair share of luck.

The Ike Williams-Ronnie James fight proved to me that Solomons had the luck that had always deserted Sydney Hulls when Hulls attempted to stage a super open-air tournament. It nearly always rained when Syd took his boxing outside. So much so that he lost complete confidence in open-air tournaments and most of his top-liners were later staged indoors at Wembley or Harringay.

For two days before the Williams-James fight it rained cats and dogs in Cardiff. It didn't ease up on the morning of the fight. It poured at the weigh-in, and when I strolled to the Cardiff ground at 4 o'clock it was still raining. My shoes became heavy as I walked across the pitch.

"You'll never get away with it to-night," I told Solomons back at the Angel Hotel. "Don't worry," he replied putting on his famous big smile which makes him look like Old Sol himself, "the sun will shine to-night."

I don't believe Solomons really thought he would see the sun shine. I reckon he was a sick man at heart but, as always, he managed to ward off the blues—one of the reasons he is always good company. By 5.20 the rain had stopped, and at 6.30 the sun actually broke through a blue patch among the clouds and shone. There was a red sunset over Cardiff that night.

So far, Solomons' luck with the weather has held. It has rained the day before. It has occasionally rained on the day of a big fight, but never has the weather ruined one of his open-air tournaments.

From America he has imported some of the world's best fighters . . . Gus Lesnevich, Joe Baksi, Lee Savold, Sugar Ray Robinson, Joey Maxim. His greatest ambition was to bring Joe Louis to England to defend his world heavyweight championship against Bruce Woodcock. These plans were shattered in April 1947, when Baksi smashed Woodcock's jaw and really started the beginning and the end of Bruce's career. Had Woodcock not fallen for the Sucker punch that night, he may well have beaten the huge American who never did anything outstanding afterwards.

Had Woodcock beaten Baksi in 1947, Solomons would have realised his ambition by staging a Louis-Woodcock undisputed heavyweight title slam at White City later that year. It doesn't really matter, however, because Bruce wouldn't have lasted many rounds with the Brown Bomber.

Mister Boxing will claim he once staged a world heavyweight title bout in England. That was in 1950 when Lee Savold stopped Woodcock in four rounds at White City, but although the British Boxing Board of Control recognised the bout as such because Louis had retired in the meantime, a more fitting champion was Ezzard Charles, who had beaten Jersey Joe Walcott for the vacant title, and who later in 1950 out-pointed Louis when the Brown Bomber attempted his come-back.

The success of Solomons is partly due to the fact that no obstacle seems too great. I don't think any boxing writer in the country believed he was capable of getting Sugar Ray Robinson to defend his world middleweight crown against our own

Randy Turpin in 1951 . . . especially as Robinson was asking for £30,000 and Solomons was committed to an indoor arena— the large Earls Court Exhibition Hall capable of holding only 18,000 compared with 50,000 at White City. However, he worked out his plan and descended on an unsuspecting Robinson who was mixing business with pleasure in Paris, and offered Sugar Ray £28,000. The Harlem Negro couldn't resist such money and, believing Turpin to be an easy touch, accepted. That was how another world title came to England . . . although the Robinson camp were themselves pretty cute, and insisted that Turpin should first agree to give Robinson a return championship fight within ninety days should Turpin win. So the title remained in British hands for but sixty-four days.

To-day Solomons has realised most of his ambitions. He has proved that East can mix with West, because the little East End fishmonger's son now lives in a luxury flat in Regent's Park and includes among his friends the people who matter in Parliament, in show business, in racing, and in Scotland Yard. In fact, Solomons knows them all.

He is lucky to have such a good wife in Fay. She hates the limelight as much as Jack loves it. She is the only person who knows the worries as well as the fortune boxing has brought him. For only at home does Jack take off the mask which carries that big smile when everything seems to be going wrong. She alone knows how sick the fight game has sometimes made him.

The only ambition left for King Solomons is to stage a world heavyweight championship in Great Britain which will be recognised as a title fight throughout the Universe. But first he has to find some young miner, engineer or fish-porter born in these isles who is big enough to fear nothing on two legs; who has the fiery ambition to go in and fight like Jack Petersen, possesses the toughness and guts of Tommy Farr, and who can box like Len Harvey. When and if that day ever comes then Solomons will realise his dreams. But Mrs. Solomons, who spends so much time alone in their flat, isn't interested in such wild dreams. Her happiness will be fulfilled when Jack relinquishes his title of Mister Boxing . . . and settles down in some quiet spot in the sun away from the aggravations of fight managers, fighters, and the telephone calls of boxing writers . . . but when that day comes I shall really believe that leprechauns light up the runways to Shannon Airport. The fight game is in his blood.

In conclusion, you may wonder why the Butlers, having seen so many glorious coronations of pugilistic kings, and having also witnessed the inevitable, and sometimes heart-breaking, fall from the throne, should end this book with the story of a promoter. Because promoters, like fight-managers, seldom fall. And their one-big-happy-family motto is: The Champ is dead. Long live the champ! The pugilist's life is a short one, but if managers and promoters don't exactly go on for ever, they usually remain in business until they are called from this earth.

Solomons qualifies as a fistic great because he has been, and still is, a king-maker—the most successful promoter this little island has ever produced. He makes up the trio of the only three fistic showmen whose names will remain immortal in the history of pugilism . . . Rickard, Jacobs and Solomons.

Although the late Rickard and Jacobs lined their pockets with gold, as has Solomons, this doesn't alter the fact that all three have done a great deal for the sport even if it was incidental. Rickard with the aid of Dempsey gave American boxing the first million-dollar gate. Jacobs, with the help of Louis, started up a U.S. monopoly of the eight world titles. Solomons challenged that monopoly after the last war, and his enterprise and energy were mainly responsible for the world light-heavyweight and middleweight titles coming to Britain. Had we boasted of more talent, he would also have helped to bring the heavyweight, the lightweight and bantamweight crowns to Britain. In short, King Solomons has done well, not only for himself, but also for the Boxing Empire which he, undoubtedly, rules.